One Day
is Now

One Day
is Now

A Financial Planning Guide for Living Well Today
Without Sacrificing Your Future Security

MARTIN TURBIN

RETHINK PRESS

First published in Great Britain 2015
by Rethink Press (www.rethinkpress.com)

Contents

Foreword

Life isn't a destination; life is a journey. And our goal should be to enjoy the journey. That's why *the purpose of investment advice should be not just to improve people's financial security but also their quality of life.* The author of this book, Martin Turbin, CFP^{cm}, shares his holistic process to help his clients do that.

I met Martin about five years ago when he inquired about my business development services for client-centred financial advisors. He was eager to go beyond his product and technical training to become a client-centred advisor. Although he was committed to adding more value than the typical broker or advisor, he didn't know exactly how to do that. He told me that he wanted to help his clients make informed decisions about their personal finances and to make a positive difference in their lives. So, I agreed to help him design and build a client-centred financial, retirement, and estate planning business.

I gave Martin permission and encouragement to listen to his clients more deeply: to understand their hearts, their minds, and their passions; not just their money. As he connected with his clients' goals, dreams, and concerns, he started seeing beyond the numbers to the impact that his advice had on their lives. Eventually, he developed his six-step life and wealth optimisation process.

Apparently the work we did made an impact, because Martin decided to share his insights and strategies with others. As I read this book I was delighted to discover that the advice in it is almost perfectly aligned with my philosophy. The book's message is that money is important, but only as a resource to support the 'good life'. Most people define *success* by keeping score in only one dimension, money. But, I believe success should be defined by many dimensions, most importantly the amount of health and happiness we experience.

Instead of starting with a product or strategy or even goals, Martin starts by helping his clients' develop a positive vision of their future. Then he works backwards from the 'ideal future' to determine what resources his clients will need to support it. Once Martin understands what his clients want to accomplish and experience, what their priorities are, and what they want to avoid, he can give them much more valuable advice. Finally he helps his clients identify and implement the best strategies to transform their vision into reality. Compared to traditional retirement planning, his process is faster, easier, and more enjoyable.

But most of us aren't clear about what will make us happy. So, we pursue money, possessions, and other things that don't enhance our quality of life. Or we live beneath our means and deny ourselves simple pleasures because we don't know what the future will bring. That is one of the best things about this book; it helps readers determine how much they can spend each year, without ever having to worry about outliving their money.

With this book, Martin, demonstrates how a client-centred financial planner can raise the bar to add meaningful value for his investors. His conversational style make this book a joy to read. It's a key resource that provides a framework for defining and planning for a long, healthy, prosperous, and fulfilling "re-inspirement."

Everyone who wants a more stress-free, fulfilling, and prosperous life should read this book. You'll learn about the good life; what it is, how much it costs, and how to achieve it. Martin's content and questions create a framework for thinking about and living *your best possible life—with the resources you have.*

The advice Martin shares in this book will help you build wealth and retire in comfort—with confidence. I hope you enjoy reading this book and encourage you to apply his strategies and advice.

Steve Moeller

President of American Business Visions, LLC and Author of Endorphinomics: *The Science of Human Flourishing*

Introduction

One Day Is Now is a wake-up call to people caught up in today's 'busyness'.

I hope to encourage you to step back from your busy lives and take time to reflect on where you are going and whether you are living the life you truly want. It will help you to examine what it will take for you to lead a more fulfilled and satisfying life. It will provide a step by step process that will give you the confidence needed to set and achieve your most cherished goals. I will assist you in this process by providing you with a number of free financial planning resources.

My Story

I grew up in the 1970s in an average community and it's fair to say I had very little financial knowledge. Like a lot of people back then, I left school at the age of 16 with no clear idea of what I wanted to do with my career. I was fairly good at maths, so I drifted into my first job working in the accounts department of a large London insurance broker. By the time I was in my mid-20s, I began to realise I was in the wrong job. I just couldn't get excited by it and I felt like life was passing me by. I knew I couldn't stay in accounts for the rest of my working life so after some soul searching I ended up taking a personality profile assessment in London. This confirmed to me I was in the wrong career and I really needed to make some changes in my life. I decided I should pursue a career as a financial advisor since it seemed more suited to my personality profile which said 'You should be in sales'. In those days giving financial advice was regarded as a sales job. Of course, these days, *sales* is almost a dirty word in the financial world.

I found this transition quite difficult at first, having been in a back office role my entire working life so far. I started my new career with the now disbanded London Life, at the time one of the oldest insurance companies in the UK, which had been established for over 200 years and so had a financial pedigree almost second to none. It was a great company to work for and I received an excellent training. But something still didn't feel right. My gut was telling me I still had more to offer but I couldn't put my finger on why I felt uncomfortable. Then one day, it dawned on me: whilst I was very good at my job I realised I was working in a partial environment, recommending products and services supplied by just the one company – my employer. What I really wanted was to offer truly independent advice and I had already begun to feel some of our competitors' financial products were better suited to the clients I was advising. It was time to move on again because I had a thirst for knowledge and wanted to expand my horizons. I was truly captivated by the world of finance but I recognised I still had gaps in my knowledge and needed more experience if I were to pursue my dream career as an independent financial advisor.

So, in 1992, with very little investment knowledge, I was offered a new job with an independent firm. I spent most of my first year learning. I wasn't prepared to start offering advice until I felt I truly knew what I was talking about. I studied and read everything I could lay my hands on to do with investing and as a result, learned a great deal about how the investment world operated. This was when the Government was introducing new schemes for people to invest in, such as Personal Equity Plans (PEPs). I immersed myself in these new arrangements and taught myself everything I could. I must have made an impression on my colleagues because, after a while, the older and much more experienced advisors were approaching me, a young man in my late 20s, asking 'These new PEPs, what are they all about, which do you think is a good one?'

I was enjoying my job and felt I was really giving my clients a great service. It was, after all, what I had previously dreamt of – fully Independent Financial Advice.

But something *still* wasn't right, something was missing and I began to get that familiar gut feeling that made me feel I needed to move on. I still couldn't help thinking there must be a better way of serving my clients and making more of an impact on their future lives. The job I was looking for – that of a lifestyle financial planner – just didn't really exist at that time, while these days it's a much more accepted and well-known term. But I had this drive to explore my potential and that feeling just wouldn't go away. I had to follow my instinct.

In 1998, I took the plunge and started my own firm in Brentwood, Essex. My goal was to help everyday people make smart decisions about their money. I felt my main strengths were a well-developed knowledge of financial planning, an ability to explain complex subjects in plain English and a burning desire to do things in a better way for clients. This is what my clients wanted from me – good, solid advice in language they could grasp. Today, I am a Certified Financial Planner^{cm} – one of only 1,000 registered in the UK – and I pride myself on delivering a highly personalised, client focused service to my clients.

One day really is now

Most of us are living lives of quiet desperation. We are burnt out, stressed and more asset-rich and time-poor than at any other time in history. We are living in the most incredible times. This era has been described as 'the golden age of opportunity' and yet most of us are putting off living the life we have dreamt about until we get old.

When we do retire, we worry about whether we can afford to do any of those things we once dreamt about. Now our concerns are 'Will I run out of money?' or 'What if I need to pay for care in the final chapter of my life?' and a host of other worries that stop us enjoying those golden years we have waited our whole lives for. We act as if our lives will go on for ever, reassuring ourselves by saying 'one day I'll do this' or 'one day I will do that'. I'm here to tell you 'one day is now!'

These fears and our innate ability to procrastinate cause us to hang on to more of our money than we are ever likely to need and many of us go to our graves with our music still in us. In my 25 years as a Financial Adviser and planner I have witnessed many cases of people leaving it too late. My client base is typically in their mid-50s and above. From a wide range of backgrounds, they're close to, or at, retirement. On the whole, they're all fairly prudent and fairly cautious with their money. They've made it or inherited it and they don't want to lose it. They may be going through some sort of transition and have identified the need to review their finances with an independent financial adviser.

Take the elderly lady, now in care, whose thrifty husband amassed a large amount of money by saving hard all his life. He passed away suddenly, shortly after retiring, leaving his wife with a huge nest egg and no one to enjoy it with.

Or the Company Director who maxed out his pension contributions, deferring all fun and enjoyment until after he retired. He also passed away unexpectedly within 18 months of retiring. There have been countless other examples over the years.

With so many financial services to choose from these days - on demand via the internet and with more confusing government legislation and regulations in place - the world of personal investments is becoming more daunting year on year. Fortunately there is a practical and elegant solution to this problem. It's called the financial lifeplan.

One Day Is Now will show you how you can create a plan with or without the help of a Certified Financial Planner[cm].

No financial plan is of much value if you are not in good health so while this is not a book on health, the first chapter covers some basics which I have found to be essential for the full enjoyment of my own life.

The next six chapters describe the six-stage financial planning process I use for my clients, with great effect.

The vision discovery session is a bit like a goal-setting workshop where you will be guided through a series of questions designed to get you thinking about all the things you would like to do during the rest of your lives. Sometimes people need to reconnect with their dreams, many of which they have put to one side and almost forgotten.

Then comes the reality check session where you will be shown how to test the likelihood of your goals becoming a reality by using free online software to create different scenarios. You choose those scenarios with the best chance of coming to fruition. These will become the goals on which your financial life plan will focus.

I will then walk you through the process for creating a written action plan for achieving the goals you've identified and through the procedure for implementing your plan by either choosing a suitable Financial Adviser or selecting your own investments and financial products. I will also provide you with free access to online risk profiling software, so you can assess for yourself your own risk tolerance score and then select investments which match your individual profile.

This main section of the book ends with a chapter setting out the process for monitoring and adjusting the financial life plan at regular intervals to help make sure it stays on track.

We conclude with two chapters on investing. The first examines the overwhelming academic evidence to support the viewpoint that active management of investments doesn't work.

This is followed by a chapter on how to avoid expensive mistakes when investing by understanding how not to let your emotions get the better of you when markets inevitably fall.

It's not my goal here to tell you which investments to buy. However, after reading this book you will have a better understanding in making those decisions, where to start and what types of investments may be right for you. Ultimately, the decisions you make are yours, but wouldn't this be a much more rewarding process if you could approach it better-informed and able to ask yourself (and your adviser if you choose to appoint one) the right questions? You may be surprised by the answers. Whatever they are, use this book as an opportunity to plan for your future so you don't end up looking back on your life with any sense of regret.

Chapter 1

Health Before Wealth

If I describe a freshly-baked apple pie with a sugary-coated crust, straight from the oven and served with lashings of fresh custard, I bet it sounds pretty tempting and tasty. But should you really eat it…?

Right now you might be thinking 'Hang on a minute, have I picked up the wrong book? I thought this was all about wealth management, not *health* management!' But in my experience, the two go hand-in-hand and I believe this is something so important it can't be ignored. At the risk of making a very bold statement right from the beginning:

If you haven't got good health then none of the rest of this book will be much use to you.

Not only am I writing with the benefit of my wealth of financial planning experience, this book is also based on my personal experience – and I want to share with you a little of my own story to help demonstrate the link between having good health and managing your wealth. I'm not about to tell you the best way to manage your money is to get up in the morning and run a marathon, swim the English Channel or climb Mount Everest. But after reading this book I want you to believe that life really is for living to the full – and you simply cannot do this without good health. The one thing I cannot guarantee you is that following my advice in this area will automatically exempt you from ill health; not even the greatest doctor or medical expert can do that. However, I would ask you to take a step back and take a critical look at your lifestyle and ask yourself:

'Could I really live longer and still have enough money to enjoy my life? Am I doing everything I possibly can, or anything at all, to at least give myself a chance of better health and the chance to enjoy my wealth in the future?'

Because without good health, once you've reached your mid 50s and beyond, it's so much more difficult to enjoy your wealth. It's hard to imagine living the life of your dreams whilst being 50 pounds overweight for example!

So perhaps the first and best investment you can make right now is in yourself and your well-being.

We're all living longer

You don't have to be a scientist to find evidence that these days we are all living longer. Even Life Insurance Companies produce a completely different set of mortality tables than they did, say, 30 years ago. But of course, that doesn't necessarily mean we're going to enjoy those extra years! And shouldn't we all be able to look forward to a thoroughly enjoyable retirement and make the most of these longer life expectancies. But to succeed in this area we need to take care of ourselves, and unfortunately this is not always that easy to do.

That's because our pace of life is faster than ever. We're busier than at any other time in human history and as a result many of us neglect our health. We say we will start to do better once we have reached a certain level in life, maybe an income level, or some level of achievement with which we feel we have finally succeeded.

The trouble is all this 'busyness' has also made us the most stressed generation in history. Many of us choose harmful and inappropriate responses to stress such as alcohol, over-eating, obesity or caffeine. All these abuses contribute to a feeling of burn out.

There is an epidemic of diseases and illnesses related to stress and 21st-century life. High blood pressure or hypertension is virtually the accepted norm for the over 50s and instead of taking steps to reduce this naturally, most of us turn to our doctors who readily prescribe drugs to address the problem.

This enables us to ignore what we are doing wrong and keep doing whatever we were doing, whether drinking alcohol every day or shoving high fat foods down our throats.

I'm not trying to criticise doctors – it's simply that our healthcare system can't keep up. Doctors don't have the time to sit down with every patient and explain the steps they could take to improve their health, so they dispense pills instead. Their focus is almost entirely on cure rather than prevention through education.

If we want to enjoy a high-quality life in retirement we have to take charge of our own wellbeing and put our health first. After all what good is having the largest bank account of all your family and friends if you can't even walk up the stairs?

Of course, this is easier said than done. It takes a lot of will power, determination and recognition (and sometimes this can be painful) to make changes to our lives. But every year, many of us say just that! It's time for change. For most of us, January 1 heralds a new beginning: but how many of us make that annual list of resolutions, determined to make changes in our lives, hit the gym hard for the first three weeks of the year, eat more healthily and then, just a few days later, head back to the old treadmill (not the gym version) and return to our old ways?

I was just like that. Over the last 25 years I've worked hard at building myself a successful business with a portfolio of great clients who come to me for financial planning advice, worried about their future spending and how they can make the most of their investments to enjoy their dream retirement. Along the way, I've also been lucky enough to eat out at really good restaurants, to take several foreign holidays every year and socialise regularly with more than the odd glass of wine! I'm also lucky in that I have a wonderful partner and family. It all sounds very idyllic, I'm sure, but there was an important part of my life that had got way out of balance – my health. I'd been feeling my energy dropping for months and had put it down to my age, but on January 1 2015, when I was… 51, I finally decided to take stock. I was 42 pounds overweight; despite being only 5ft 8ins tall, I needed trousers with a 40-inch waist; I couldn't really be very active without getting short of breath; I felt lethargic all the time – and on most mornings, I really didn't feel much like getting out of bed at all to go to work.

Something was clearly wrong and I needed to make some big changes to my lifestyle. Just as clients come to me looking for advice about how they can change their finances, I decided to consult a personal trainer to help get me back into shape. I also made changes to my diet because I knew that if I didn't do something about it, I could end up having a heart attack, stroke or becoming gravely ill as I got older. I didn't want to be one of those people who retire and then through ill health can't enjoy it, or worse, die. Simply by making more effort and looking after yourself now should help reduce the risks of contracting some of the more chronic conditions we associate with old age – meaning that you and your family can enjoy your health and wealth for a lot longer. It goes without saying, if you are thinking of taking dramatically more exercise or changing to a healthier diet, make sure you speak with your doctor or have a medical check-up first.

Don't leave it too late

Over the years, I've known so many couples who didn't come to me first for financial advice but who had been saving, saving, saving for their golden years of retirement. Then, when (usually) the husband, retires, he dies soon afterwards and their golden years together never happen, leaving the grieving widow to adjust to a new life. I'm not suggesting that in these circumstances the causes of death are all attributable to a poor diet and an unhealthy lifestyle. Often these matters are completely out of our control.

'One day' is now. Especially as most of us treat our lives as if it's a two-week holiday: you arrive, it's all great, you have no cares in the world and the first week seems to go on forever. But after that first Saturday, the following week disappears in no time at all and, in the blink of an eye, you're on the plane back home wondering 'Where the heck did that last week go?' If you're over 50, like me, then you're already in the second week of your life, metaphorically speaking, and you're wondering 'Where did all that time go?'

So, if this does apply to you, now is the time to start doing something about it. That does mean you have to consider some harsh realities, such as the two fundamental problems in dying with too much money which are:

1. Your family might end up paying a big chunk of inheritance tax

2. You could have enjoyed your retirement a great deal more by doing more with your money instead of leaving it to HMRC!

Why we miss out

Over the years, I've noticed people seem terrified of actually enjoying their years of retirement. Many of the clients I have advised have been overly worried about spending money on themselves or giving it to loved ones now because they're concerned they might need it to pay for the dreaded nursing home fees sometime in the not-so-distant future. They believe they won't have sufficient funds to cope with any catastrophe that might come along. I also believe that it's a hangover of our parents' very prudent mentality, acquired while they were growing up during or just after the Second World War; they saved up, they paid off their mortgages and generally looked after their money in very traditional ways. And this mentality has been passed down to their children – now in their late 50s and beyond – and it's a very hard mind-set to shake off, to persuade them that it's OK to spend their income and to draw down their capital. But if you simply hold on to your money in the old traditional ways, it's not serving you or your loved ones in any meaningful way. Plus, if you're not looking after your health and you die soon after retirement, then nobody wins except, as I have said, possibly the tax man.

The result is that people leave far too much money in the bank or hold on to their equity (in property). But with the right planning, they could have done so much more with their money and led a much richer, more fulfilled life. This approach to wealth management simply doesn't make sense. The main problem is that people don't have a proper financial plan incorporating a life-long cashflow forecast. The plan and forecast are the starting point in getting clarity and confidence about the future. Another, smaller, part of the problem is lack of education about how you can structure your investments and financial affairs to get the most out of them in your retirement. In my firm we create a financial plan and lifelong cashflow forecast for every client, using state-of-the-art software. I then show clients how much their lifestyle is likely to cost having taken account of their most cherished goals and factoring in potential future catastrophes (such as needing to enter into long-term care). It's essential you feel secure that whatever you decide to do today with your money won't cripple you in retirement. The financial plan and lifelong cashflow forecast should be of tremendous help to you in achieving peace of mind in this area. We will discuss how to create both and supply free tools to allow you to do this for yourself later in this book.

Get and stay active

I'm not about to start offering you any prescriptive advice about taking exercise. After all, I'm a Certified Financial Planner[cm], not a fitness expert, so if you are inspired to take up an active exercise plan after reading this book, then make sure you receive a thorough health assessment first from your doctor or a trained medical expert. As indeed I did when I decided to stop putting it off with my usual excuse, 'I'll get round to it one day' before I realised that 'One day is now'.

As a result, what I can tell you is that I've undergone a substantial transformation in my life. Before January 2015 I was typical of many people my age – I ate too much, probably drank too many glasses of wine with dinner and didn't exercise nearly enough. In fact, the exercise I did do – pretty half-heartedly – was mainly racquet sports where I was likely to injure myself and often did! So I gradually piled on maybe one or two pounds each year without taking much notice until I had that 40-inch waist and weighed in at 15 stone 3 pounds, the heaviest I've ever been.

At 51 years old I'd convinced myself that all my problems were due to my age. But there are loads of people, many of them 10 to 20 years older than me, who are fit. I've lost tennis matches to many of them!

So, it really was a bit rich of me to tell my clients, 'One day is now, don't save it all until tomorrow, go and enjoy your lives' when I wasn't taking my own advice. Guiding my clients through their ideal retirement requires me to be at my best at all times, mentally alert, highly personable and offering them the best possible service. My clients, rightly, have very high expectations of me and I am passionate about delivering this. But prior to my realisation that all was not well with my health, I'll admit I'd stopped taking appointments in the late afternoons and even avoided after work events which could have been useful to me – because I simply didn't have the energy. I have no doubt the way I was feeling was having a negative impact on my business and turnover. When I finally realised this and what was happening to me, I knew then it was time to make some positive changes quickly.

I'm still not quite there yet and it's very much still a work in progress. But I can see and feel the differences after only six months: I've lost two stone, dropped two trouser sizes and I absolutely love the workout regime I do as well as the healthy diet I've adopted. I've discovered it's actually pleasant not to feel full all the time. Not everyone will want to engage the services of a personal trainer like I have done, but there is a lot we can all do to take the first steps towards a healthier lifestyle (following a fitness assessment) to improve our health by even a simple thing, such as walking more every day or choosing a chicken salad instead of chicken and chips.

However, I can honestly say I feel I transformed in just six months after taking more exercise and eating healthier foods in four key areas:

- I am mentally more alert
- I am more confident
- I feel as good as I did 10 years ago
- I am free of acid reflux (a debilitating condition that completely saps energy which I used to experience almost every time I ate)

I can now concentrate far better on being the best adviser I am capable of being for my clients. I'm not avoiding those afternoon meetings or social events because I am too tired, and I've also regained a sense of vitality every morning when I wake up. All because I made a conscious decision to make some positive changes in my life.

I haven't stopped making changes, either. For example, I work out pretty hard and I make sure I push myself gradually as I progress. My personal trainer concentrates on the resistance work (with weights), and on alternate days I do some cardio exercises, such as a spin class. I took my inspiration from a book called *Younger Next Year* by Chris Crowley and Dr Henry Lodge, aimed at 50-80 year olds; I would recommend this to anyone who wants to make sure they are in the best condition to enjoy this period in their lives.

Since I've adopted this new exercise and dietary regime, I pass on to my clients the massive improvement it's made to my enjoyment of life. It's so important if they are going to get the best out of their financial plan. It's not my place to suggest you lose weight, give up smoking or take more exercise – but I am passionate about helping you live your best retirement so am keen to share my story in the hope it might inspire you, even a little, to take good care of your own health.

I'd like to think, therefore, that the starting point for my financial advice begins with a more personal approach. Normally I'd ask a new client what their goals and dreams are, what they would like their life to look like five years from now, but I increasingly point out that the one thing they need above all else to enjoy all the great things that could be planned for their retirement is energy.

Eat right (garbage in, garbage out)

You might have all the money in the world and you might exercise hard every day but if you keep feeding your body the wrong fuel, you're missing a huge part of the equation. We're all tempted to eat far too much fat in our diets and I for one would use a meal out as a reward for a successful day or week at work. It was rarely a healthy one! I never did the sensible thing such as rewarding myself with a good healthy treat such as a walk in the country or a swim and jacuzzi. I would often snack or eat large meals and convince myself it was all right because I was eating healthily, but there was nothing very healthy about piling my food up on my plate like a pyramid.

This all changed when I started monitoring my portion sizes and thanks to my current exercise plan, I'm drinking about three litres of water per day, something we should all do but few of us manage. Similarly, we tend not to eat anywhere near enough vegetables and even when they are included in the meal they are often only done so as a token gesture on the side of a plate loaded with meat and refined carbohydrates such as white rice or pasta. We all know it should probably be the other way round where the plate is two thirds made up of vegetables, but many of us carry on just the same.

Of course, it's always the bad foods that appeal the most: from Indian takeaways to the ready meals in supermarkets, from the highly-processed to the highest in fat content, they are readily available, convenient, relatively cheap and tempting. However, I've not stopped myself from eating out and I still reward myself. But my habits have changed. I usually take a day off from the exercise regime once a week and what I've noticed now is that when I get to my treat day, I actually don't want that huge plate of steak and chips or the apple pie and custard. My new habits are now so ingrained that my brain has retrained itself when it comes to the type of reward I want and portion sizes. You just need to stick with the healthy regime long enough for your new habits to lock in. Most experts reckon it takes about 21 days to form a new habit so if you can get through this most difficult period your likely to have cracked it. From my own experience I can promise you it's well worth the effort. Nowadays, I don't believe you can beat a colourful salad topped with some chicken, lean meat or fish. All your carbohydrate needs are contained in the vegetables, tomatoes or salad. Think about it: a car doesn't run any worse just because the tank is only half full, and we're no different. We can run very well on half a tank so even that phrase 'full up now' conjures up an image in my mind of feeling bloated and uncomfortable. It's hardly the best way to feel if you want to enjoy life to the maximum; it's a bit like how you feel just after you had your Christmas dinner. It's absolutely fine on Christmas day but you wouldn't want to feel like that every day.

The same principles I now follow can apply to your health and to your wealth. Retraining your brain to think differently about both means you still have enough room for that occasional special treat. So by all means, have that apple pie now if you want it!

Chapter 2

Discovering Your Vision

'Would you tell me, please, which way
I ought to go from here?'
'That depends a good deal on where you want to get to.'
'I don't much care where –'
'Then it doesn't matter which way you go.'
Lewis Carroll, *Alice in Wonderland*

Know where you are heading

If you don't know where you are headed in life, don't be surprised if you're not really that happy or end up in a place where you're not happy. In this chapter I'll be setting out my simple plan to help you rediscover an aspect of your life that you've probably put to one side or even forgotten about. That aspect is contained in your dreams for your future. Now ask yourself:

'Am I living my life by accident or by design?'

If you answered 'by accident' it's at this point worth spending some time in designing your life the way you want it to be. It's all too easy to lurch from one day to the next by being reactive, as opposed to proactive, in terms of planning your life. If you know where you are heading, that's a good starting point, even if, like an aircraft or ship, much of the time you stray from the path and end up off course. These vessels always end up at the right destination by making course corrections along the way because they always know exactly where they are heading.

In the same way, your goals are destinations in your future and they will help inspire you to live the life of your dreams by pulling you in the right direction, even if you get off track some of the time. The key is to know where you are heading so you need to have goals. If you are ever off-track (and you will be a lot of the time) you can make adjustments as needed but without goals you are bound to fail as you will always miss a target you cannot see.

Committing your goals to paper has been illustrated by a study, which was apparently carried out at Harvard in the 1960s, to be a very effective method of *achieving* them. This study is said to be based on a group of MBA students who were asked if they had set written goals for their future:

- 3% reported they had written down their goals
- 10% said they had goals generally in mind but had not written them down
- 87% had no specific goals at all.

Fast forward 10 years and the same students were interviewed again and the results were astounding!

The 10% of students who had goals generally in mind were earning, on average, twice as much as the 87% who had no goals at all.

But the much more impressive statistic was that the 3% percent who had written goals were earning, on average, 10 times more than the other 97% combined.

This is a staggering example of the power of having written goals. It dramatically proves that having worthy goals gives you an almost unbelievable advantage over others with no specific goals or purpose in life. Having goals that excite and energise you provides you with a sense of purpose and motivates you to live the best life you can.

Whilst it is critically important to have goals, it's of equal importance to ensure your goals are balanced. For example, you would not regard someone who had achieved great success in the area of his finances as successful if he was so out of shape he couldn't walk up the stairs, or if he worked seven days a week, 12 hours a day and had no friends or social life. Often you meet people like this who are very successful in one particular area - usually financial. Perhaps this has a lot to do with our highly materialistic western culture but often it's health, family or spirituality that are being neglected. Sadly these people are often complete disasters in others areas of their lives, perhaps alcoholics or going through a particularly ugly divorce. This is why I recommend setting goals in the eight key areas of your life:

- Health
- Financial
- Career/Business
- Relationship
- Spiritual

- Mental
- Family
- Lifestyle

Setting goals in each of these areas should help ensure you achieve a good degree of balance in your life and much greater happiness, in the long run, than just achieving massive success in one or two areas would bring you.

Give yourself permission to dream

Before I begin any financial planning consultation with new clients I ask them to tell me their dreams for the future. It's not unusual for them to find this question difficult to answer at first as their dreams may have been long forgotten or pushed to one side indefinitely as they have been accustomed to dealing with life's 'more pressing' issues. I have a real and important purpose in asking them what might seem to be a strange, unexpected question as I want to create a financial plan which reconnects them with their most cherished dreams. This in my view is the true purpose of proper financial planning.

Often they need quite a bit of help in realising or remembering what it is they want to do with their lives and, like the rest of us, have suppressed, forgotten or buried many of the desires that they held when they were younger. This is entirely understandable since real life often gets in the way of dreams: for example, keeping down a job, getting married, buying a house, and raising children – the list goes on. In my experience, the biggest problem people have with their goals is they are usually too small. We are often far too conservative in this regard.

I don't happen to think dreams are just unattainable flights of fancy. I believe your dreams (i.e. your hopes for the future) can tell you a lot about where you are now in your mind-set and are essential in helping understand what you want your financial plan to achieve for you; what it is you *truly* want from the future. Only then is it possible to take a step back and look objectively at how you might achieve them. As the free-thinking American author, Henry Thoreau (1817-1862) once said:

'*Go confidently in the direction of your dreams! Live the life you've imagined.*'

Which is precisely what I'd urge you to consider first *before* making any *emotional* decisions about what you *can't* afford to do. Therefore, throughout this chapter, I'll be encouraging you to think about your wealth in a different kind of way.

Your wealth is there to assist and support you in living the life of your dreams. There is little point in having a plan which has the goal of beating the market, whatever that means. That is investing for the sake of it and how inspiring is that? It's not really even a goal at all. A true goal might be to enjoy a fantastic, healthy retirement with two foreign holidays a year, safe in the knowledge you will never run out of money for the rest of your life. Your plan needs to be directed towards achieving the life you want. Your very best, happiest life possible.

Having vision is not the same as identifying goals

If you've ever seen the film *The Wolf of Wall Street* you'll know that its central character is based on the real life New York Stock Exchange trader Jordan Belfort. It's a film that charts his rise and fall on Wall Street through aggressive pitching, winning deals and leading an excessive and decadent lifestyle. One of its central questions is 'was Belfort truly happy?' It's not my place to speculate on that, but one thought I find interesting that Belfort has raised since the making of the film (during a podcast with Andrew Ferebee who interviews high achievers) is that he believes too many people set goals without having a clear vision first. He clarifies this by adding that, in his opinion, the people who go around setting goals and accomplishing them without having a vision are usually negative, because they hit a goal and then move on to the next one without having a higher purpose, which is demotivating.

In business, identifying and communicating a clear vision is one of the most important functions a business leader can perform. The same is true when applied to you in your personal life. In Chapter 4 we will examine in more detail the specific process in setting your realistic goals. But here I want to be clear about what it means to have a vision, which is often confused with goal setting.

Examples of goals:

- To lose 10 pounds in weight
- To help pay for your grandchild's education
- To take a dream holiday to Australia

Examples of vision (that match the goals from above):

- To live a healthy, well-balanced life
- To help provide the best possible start in life for your family
- To feel truly alive and living a joyful life

Your vision will be an idealised picture of the future you want to create and should embody your values and your view of the future without being too generic. Your vision can also change over time. The point is to have one so you know why you're doing what you do, and you're happier doing it.

Visioning is the first step in your strategic planning towards your financial future. A vision shared by you and your partner/spouse is both motivating and empowering. Without a strong vision, your strategic plans cannot be described properly since there is no guiding principle or ideal to plan. A vision will help you decide what to do and what not to do in the time approaching, for example your retirement.

A good vision will:

- identify your direction and purpose
- be credible
- require your enthusiasm and thus encourages commitment to your goals
- be well articulated and easily understood
- fit with your lifestyle choices

For example, if your goal is to lose weight, it can be very helpful to imagine yourself looking thin. It's more powerful to create a picture of what you *want* than struggling with what you want to resist. You can more easily sustain your energy and commitment. However, even though you have a powerful picture, losing weight is a goal, not a vision. Unless it is connected with a vision of something greater, like a healthy body or positive self-image, you are likely to put the weight back on.

Therefore, having a Vision is not about finding the path, it's about the destination. As you take each step, the next step becomes clear as long as you stay focused on your vision.

> '*You don't have to see the whole staircase,*
> *just take the first step.*'
> **Martin Luther King, Jr.**

Your Vision Discovery is designed to create positive emotions and link you directly to the things and experiences you want most from your money. By getting you to focus your attention on a positive future, the Vision Coaching session will create a feeling of elation and excitement about your future. This happens when you anticipate achieving your most cherished dreams and aspirations — and solving your most pressing financial concerns.

Your Vision Discovery

Before you start with your voyage of discovery I encourage you to be more ambitious than you normally allow yourself to be. Now is not the time to hold back so really indulge yourself in some blue sky thinking. You'll be able to get realistic later, but right now I want you to shoot for the stars and get your very best vison of your life committed to paper.

When we arrive at this stage of my process with a client, I often see them visibly lighten up as they discover how I am going to help them achieve exciting things with their lives that they had not imagined beforehand. The clients I have dealt with over the years are typical of a lot of people: they've buried most of their goals and are just plodding along doing what they've always done. They struggle to know what to spend their money on because they are so out of touch with their goals or they think they are unachievable. As a result, they end up in a permanently pessimistic state in which they don't want to disappoint themselves by even thinking about the future (or even the possibility of enjoying their full potential) because they simply haven't yet discovered how to use their capital in this way.

But my process begins to open up their minds to spending some of their capital on achieving their dreams in a carefully managed way. At the same time it ensures they retain more than enough money to live on. It starts with confusion and ends with the revelation they often should be spending *more* money, not less. Of course this is not always the case and sometimes, in order to live the life of their dreams, a client may need to reduce spending when, for example, they want to leave a highly-paid job they detest in order to follow their dream. However, in my practice, the clients I tend to work with are usually already successful financially and have all the money they will ever need. My purpose is then to help them get clear about how to use these resources to help them achieve their best lives (whatever that may mean for them).

British people in particular are often so prudent it takes a change in perception before they can get comfortable with spending their own money. No matter how small that change is, it can have a significant impact on their future happiness. Whether it's being able to afford a housekeeper or a Ferrari, it's not the value of the end result in cash terms, it's the qualitative effect of these changes that makes the biggest impact on the person/family. So it doesn't matter whether it's £5,000 or £500,000 extra that they realise they suddenly have access to, it still remains considerably more than they originally thought they could access and for many of my clients, this is as much an emotional discovery as it is a financial one.

To help my clients reach their Vision Discovery, I ask them to answer some questions which I've listed below for you to consider and then answer. Some of you might look at these questions and think 'I don't know how to answer that' or 'I don't know whether it is going to cost me more or less'. Quite possibly, you'll not be able to find a response at this stage to all these questions. But the important step now is for you to think about all your potential future options if you are planning or already in your retirement years. Don't worry if you can't answer all the questions just yet – I will provide you with some useful tools in the remaining chapters to help you so when you revisit the questions, you'll better equipped to respond. One such tool is some free financial planning software that will enable you stress-test your goals in order to determine how realistic they are.

You are now going to take a very exciting step in creating your ideal future. Put aside everything else, grab a cup of tea and allow yourself an uninterrupted hour or two to design your ideal life.

These are the questions I use in my practice to help my clients discover what their ideal life would look like (You can also download this form from www.turbinfp.co.uk/free-resources if you prefer not to write in the book):

Questions

1. In an ideal world, what would you like to see happen in the next chapter of your life?

2. What one or two things bring you the most energy and joy in your life?

3. What do you want more of in your life?

4. If money weren't an issue, what would you probably be doing with your time?

5. What dreams or aspirations did you have when you were younger that you would really like to reconnect with now?

6. If you knew you couldn't fail what would you probably do?

7. What stress creators are you looking forward to getting behind you?

8. Take a moment and picture yourself in the future.

   a. Where are you living?

   b. Who are you spending time with?

c. What are you doing?

d. Are you continuing to work or are you fully retired? If you are working what are you doing and how much money are you making?

e. Is it costing more or less than you are currently spending? (By roughly how much?)

f. Describe your ideal future home. Is it bigger or smaller? More or less expensive?

g. Describe your ideal future neighbourhood and community.

h. What will be the most fulfilling way to spend your time?

9. When do you want to make full time work optional?

10. Where will your income be coming from?

11. Have you considered working or consulting part time when you 'quit your real job?

12. How much would this pay?

13. Will your positive future cost more or less than your current lifestyle?

14. How much income will you need to support this lifestyle?

15. What extraordinary purchase or expenses will you have to incur to create you ideal future? (new home, son or daughter's wedding, etc.)

16. Where will the capital for these purchases come from?

17. What other personal and/or financial goals do you have?

18. What are the major challenges or issues that may prevent you from achieving your ideal future and goals?

19. How would you like to be remembered after you're gone?

20. Do you feel you have your affairs in order if something happens to you (getting hit by a bus tomorrow)?

21. If you only had one month to live, what would you do and why?

Reproduced with kind permission of Steve Moeller
(American Business Visions LLC)

Whew! I bet that was revealing for you and that was the first time in a long time you actually spent some time thinking about exactly what you want to do with your life. Did it bring up some conflicting emotions for you? Maybe even a slight feeling of guilt? Or maybe you just feel elated to have clarified your vision. Whatever feelings it brought up, don't worry. This is perfectly normal, particularly if you've been suppressing them. As we work through this book you're going to get more comfortable with living your life the way you want it but sometimes it just takes a little while to accept that this is perfectly OK and no, you are not being selfish.

If you're really struggling to get clear about your goals, remember there is no set definition of what a goal can or cannot be. Goals can be any type of dream you'd like to achieve, no matter how big or small they appear to be. The important thing is build your goals around your most cherished dreams. In the first instance, try following these three simple guidelines:

1. Write them down, otherwise they are likely to get lost or forgotten.

2. Dream big if you want to, don't hold back and filter at this stage. It doesn't matter if dreams are realistic or

not, because at this early stage the important thing is to write them down - you can have the reality check later and I will deal with this in more detail in the next chapter.

3. Make sure they are *your* goals and not someone else's or they will fail to inspire you. Or you might find, as Stephen R. Covey observed in 1989 when he published *The Seven Habits of Highly Effective People:*

'If the ladder is not leaning against the right wall, every step we take just gets us to the wrong place faster.'

Steps towards realising your vision

In order to begin bringing your vision into reality you will need to create a plan. The plan should define your purpose and reflect your core values in a way that is meaningful to you. In the process of understanding your core values you will embark on a journey of self-discovery. You are not on a mission to create or reinvent a new you. Your core values have probably been embedded within you for most of your adult life but often, due to pressures of work and family commitments, we don't take enough time to reflect on the person we really are.

Once your vision is clear in your heart and mind, it must be communicated and articulated clearly so that it becomes the *shared* vision in any partnership. Your shared vision will help you focus on the way ahead in achieving your goals. At regular intervals, remind yourself what your vision stands for – there is nothing wrong in repeating this over and over again to yourself since repetition helps keep the vision alive.

Summary

Goals are specific but vision is foresight and vision is the big picture of where you see yourself in 5-10 years' time.

Goals are measurable but it is very difficult to measure vision because vision is related to dreams and long term view. This means your goals can be both short and long term, but vision only focuses on long term view.

Goals have specific deadlines but vision does not have any specific deadline.

When you achieve your goals, you'll see the results straight away

Achieving your vision is harder to qualify – you'll only really know you're living your vision when you realise you have a sense of contentment and are happy.

Chapter 3

Determine What You Can Afford

Now you can begin the financial planning process and start to turn some of your dreams into reality. You should now be at the stage where you have identified your goals, no matter how ambitious or impossible they might seem. The good news is you've arrived at the point where you'll now do a reality check on each of them.

But what if you are like most people who are naturally conservative with your dreams and have scaled back your ambitions because you believe you'll never be able to afford them? If this is you, I'd encourage you to take another look at your goals and be brave – spend some time and blue sky your dreams. Don't worry, this won't be a frivolous exercise since this is about opening your mind to possibilities, even if some of them need to be trimmed back when you come to stress test them. Try not to hold back because you never know, something you've always dreamt of being able to do or have, but have simply blocked out of your future hopes, may be possible to achieve in some shape or another.

If, on the other hand, you have set yourself some goals that are obviously not achievable in the short term following the financial planning process, don't be disheartened. A reality check is just that – a moment to take stock and ground yourself in a managed and considered way. Making plans now, even if you discover you can't retire as soon as you'd like, will help you manage your finances and know what you can afford to spend in the future. It's a lot less stressful than retiring and suddenly worrying how long your money will last.

Once you have determined what you can afford you may be pleasantly surprised. A lot of people think this part of planning is quite dry. But when they've completed it, for many it's actually quite liberating. This chapter is about creating a plan so you will have a clearer picture of where you are going and any adjustments needed to be made in order to make your goals a reality.

Identify your expenses

One critically important piece of the jigsaw is to identify your expenses, now and in the future.

You should complete an expenditure analysis using the link at the end of this segment in which you will detail what your current life style is costing you. Remember, to take into account *everything*, not just your day-to-day expenses. Also include any significant one-offs you have planned, for example a new car or contributing to your children's wedding costs. It's important to start by knowing what you're currently spending and then what you'd like to be spending in the future. It's a process I highly recommend you go through if you want to have a plan you can believe will work for you.

I also recommend you add in an expense item I call wild living. Make this an extra 10% or so of your total expenditure. This builds in a bit of fat to allow you to have some fun and provides some breathing space for the plan in case you have underestimated any of your other expenses. It's a bit like planning a holiday and a route, allowing for some detours along the way so you can spend a little extra if you end up in a really nice place where you wanted to spend a bit more time and money. This way, you'll know you're covered.

There are five categories of expenses to consider

Basics - for example

- Council tax
- Utility bills (such as water rates, electricity, telephone/internet)
- Mortgages or rent
- Groceries
- Transport/commuting

Leisure - for example

- Annual holidays
- Trips to theatre/cinema
- Dining out Healthcare
- Fitness clubs

Luxury -for example

- Home improvements
- Holiday trip of a lifetime
- Spa treatments

Milestones - for example

- Helping your children with a deposit on their first home
- Family weddings

Legacy -for example

- Legal costs for drafting wills and lasting power of attorney

A word of warning: you may be tempted to think identifying all of the above is too much like hard work because you've never documented the information before, or you might think this process is simply too boring – or perhaps you just can't find all the information. Don't be disheartened and don't give up. It's normal to resist a bit at this part of the planning process and if you really do feel it's all too much like hard work a perfectly acceptable shortcut would be to just look at three months' bank statements and note what comes in and what goes out. The difference between the two is what you're spending each month. Then just add in a bit of wild living expenses in case you want to spend more in the future.

Of course, your wild living allowance depends on your own personal circumstances. For example, your income may be £50,000 per year and if you currently spend all of it, adding another 10% (£5,000) for wild living will have to be funded by drawing down on capital. This draw down of capital needn't be a problem so long as you can see you will still not run out of money during your lifetime. It's also worth pointing out it's not compulsory for you to spend it every year and if your investments have had an inevitable bad year you may choose to wait until they recover until you recommence the extra wild living withdrawal. Obviously spending extra capital now is likely to reduce the amount you will able to leave behind for loved ones but you may enjoy life more by giving some to them now while you're here and able to see the benefit of your generosity. I know this is what I'd prefer rather than leaving a huge pile for after I'm gone. Another added benefit of this approach is a likely reduction in Inheritance Tax (IHT) payable by your loved ones.

Now you have your expenses listed and you've included your wild living allowance let's see what your financial forecast looks like and assume for now you are not going to go broke. You may now be wondering, 'How can I plan on this scale when 'I don't know how long I will live?' It's a reasonable question. I recommend you create a plan which is based on you living until your 100th birthday! This may seem excessive and surprise you a little, but think about it: one in 10 of us are making it to this milestone already and life expectancy is increasing in every generation. Of course, there is no guarantee for each of us, but if you make your plans based on the assumption you will be gone at 90, what happens then if you carry on for another 10 years? (*Note: for any readers who have already reached their 100th birthday you may wish to extend your forecast another 5-10 years!*) But, seriously, if you have been prudent enough to plan to reach at least 100, then at least you'll have extra peace of mind you'll not be penniless the day the telegram arrives from Buckingham Palace.

The problem of Inheritance Tax

The problem of Inheritance Tax (IHT) crops up frequently with my clients, either because they haven't thought about it properly or they're worried that their estate will end up paying a large tax bill after they die. Therefore, now is a good time to work out what your options are (such as spending more money, giving some away etc.) to secure as much of your estate as possible for your children or other beneficiaries.

But saving IHT is not necessarily the only reason you may wish to consider spending more or giving more away during your lifetime. In fact many people are not particularly motivated by saving inheritance tax (especially true if you have no children). However there is perhaps an even stronger reason why you may wish to consider not having too much left over at the end of your life and that is you could be enjoying your retirement more fully by spending it on the little luxuries (or big ones!) in life that could make all the difference. The following two examples show having no plans in place at all will see a large proportion of your hard-earned wealth going straight to the Tax Man.

Example 1

The following graph is based on a widow aged 65 with a net worth of £3.8m and an IHT liability of around £1.2m. Over time and using a modest assumption of 5% growth in the value of her assets this will increase exponentially until by age 100 the liability is over £4m. With no IHT planning or increases in spending, you can clearly see that a substantial part of this lady's estate will benefit the State.

Example 2

A married couple have a £3m estate. Both Nil Rate Bands are intact so £1m is exempt from Inheritance Tax and each child receives an equal share of the estate after tax, but it is still HMRC that is the single largest beneficiary.

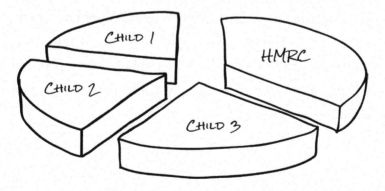

Taxman the largest beneficiary

For the most current nil-rate band IHT threshold, please use the Government web link provided at the end of this chapter.

Making your assumptions

Once you know what your desired future life style will cost you can then work backwards to calculate how much capital you will actually need. But remember, you can spend capital as well. For example, if you have £1 million in investments – and based on an assumption that they will increase in value on an annual basis at 5% -that's going to generate £50,000 a year for you. There's no need to keep the £1m intact until the day you die. You can actually draw down some of this capital on an annual basis. Obviously I'm not suggesting for one moment you go on a massive spending spree or empty your bank account and cash in all your investments in the next three years. What I'm actually suggesting is a managed drawdown of your capital over the course of the rest of your life. This requires planning and regular reviews to make sure you're not spending too quickly so that you never run out.

Tips for making your assumptions:

- Plan to live until your 100th birthday
- Don't draw down too quickly so that you fully deplete your funds
- Use conservative assumptions for growth
- Assume that one or both of you might need long-term care by the age of 80
- Adjust your assumptions to see what would happen to your future income if one of you needs care by the age of 75 and examine how this might affect your available funds
- Ask yourself, are you going to be spending more money in real terms in retirement than you are today?
- Build inflation into expense assumptions
- Update your plan annually in the light of actual information i.e. did your investments grow by more, or less, than your original assumption
- Adjust your spending accordingly

Case Study

Fred and Freda Smith – how adjusting your plans will determine what you can realistically afford:

- Fred is 55 and Freda is 53 and both are entitled to the full state pension at age 66. They have a goal of retiring when Fred is 60, and they wish to carry on spending £50k per annum.
- They have a combined income of £100k
- Their current annual expenditure is £50k.
- Fred has a personal pension worth £350k
- Freda has a personal pension worth £150k.
- They also have combined savings and investments of £150k
- Their house is valued at £750k with no mortgage

The graph below shows Fred and Freda's lifelong cashflow forecast as things stand right now. It shows that their goal to retire by 60 is unrealistic as they will run out of money by Fred's age 77 (where graph shows 'shortfall').

Cashflow Forecast 1

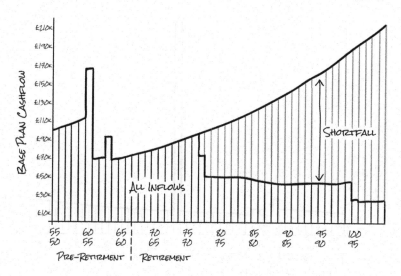

However, the next graph shows that if they revise their goal to retire at 65 and then also downsize their property at age 80, from £750k to £500k, then they will never run out of money and can carry on spending £50k until the end of their lives – in this case aged 100. This is now a realistic goal based on what they have determined they can afford.

Cashflow Forecast 2

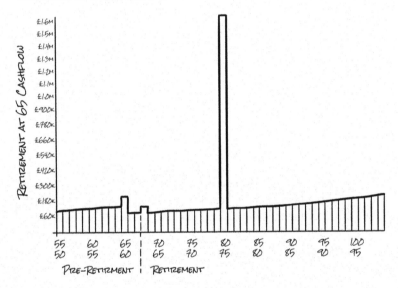

The large spike in the cashflow forecast is the release of equity from downsizing the home.

There are, of course, myriad ways they could have revised their goal i.e. retire at 60, but work part time to 70, or save more money into pensions now and still be able to retire at 60. This graph is just presented to illustrate their original goal needed revising. I recommend you play around with different scenarios like this once you have entered your data into the free financial planning software recommended in this book. Do this until you settle on a plan that feels right for *you.*

What stops most people from making this first step in determining what they can afford?

The simple answer is fear of the future since this is an unknown quantity.

A huge issue for people living in the UK is the cost of potential care fees in later life. It seems you can't pick a Sunday newspaper up without reading how much the cost of care home fees is increasing and that local authorities are taking people's homes away from them to pay for it. But with one in three of us facing the very real possibility of ending up in care, our natural instinct is to become more conservative now in order to offer some sort of security for the future. This results in us keeping our money locked safely away and putting aside any thoughts of taking an extravagant holiday just in case we might not be able to afford the care costs. This is a very valid concern. If you are a married couple, you might be asking yourself, should you plan for one or both of you having to go in care? This depends on how conservative you want to be. If you really want to be cautious, assume that both of you are going into care. One thing you know is that all your assumptions are just that – assumptions – and they are going to be wrong. You simply have to approach this process in an educated fashion on the basis that you can never predict exactly what the future will actually bring. But if you plan sufficiently and carefully enough in advance, you stand a much better chance of mitigating the effects of a potential expense, such as entering into long term care. Without such planning, your later years may be less enjoyable or harder to bear.

There is a very simple tool that will help you in determining what you can afford. It's based on the principle of:

- Needs
- Wants
- Savings

Needs are things you *must* pay no matter what: housing, food, utilities, transportation costs, insurance.

Wants are everything else: television subscriptions, restaurant meals, concert tickets, books, clothing beyond the basics, etc.

Savings are anything else left after you take care of Wants and Needs, and can be set aside for the future.

Chances are, if you've never looked at your finances in this way before, then your financial life may well be in a state of unbalance. But as you begin to identify what percentage of your money belongs in each of the above categories, you will have a clearer picture of where your money is going and you will begin to gain a more balanced view.

Case Study

Joyce Tanbury, an 80-year-old widow with no children or close relatives, now lives in a nursing home, but she retains a £2m+ investment portfolio. Her husband William was thrifty and ran a very modest home and they had never thought to spend any of their money on non-essential items, such as dream holidays or purchasing a second home. With no contacts apart from professionals, she sought my advice after her husband had passed away.

When we reviewed her and her husband's previous lifestyle, it didn't seem like there was any goal other than saving for saving's sake. Had they both contacted me whilst he was still alive I would have created a life-long cash flow forecast and been in a position to show them that they were not making the most of their wealth.

Unfortunately she now has much more money than she really needs to live out the rest of her life. She has no opportunities to spend it or enjoy it with anyone, something she and her husband could have done without being extravagant, whilst he was alive. It was clear that they, in fact, had more than enough capital during their latter years to spend on the nicer things in life and, more importantly, together.

If they had decided to spend another £10,000 pounds a year from the age of 65, would they have gone broke? No, they wouldn't. Look at all the other things they could have been doing. If only they had had the foresight to determine what they could afford in their good health before it was too late and without drawing down too heavily on their available funds, his wife would at least have some extra special memories to look back on.

I find this real life story very sad and it is examples such as this which have led me to write this book.

The obvious lesson to be learned here is that life is often shorter than you think. But for many of us, it's one of those taboos that is not discussed enough or planned in detail for any future. For people to be able to fully enjoy their lives, they ought to start doing some of what they've always wanted to do now, but they need to be able to do that without feeling guilty or concerned that they may have actually compromised their future by doing it.

Financial planning and in particular, determining what you can afford, is the process that allows you to get comfortable with that.

Useful links

https://planner.royallondon.com for free financial planning software

www.turbinfp.co.uk/free-resources for sample of the financial planning questionnaire (courtesy of Voyant UK)

https://www.gov.uk/government/publications/rates-and-allowances-inheritance-tax-thresholds for current Inheritance Tax Nil Rate Band allowance

https://www.gov.uk/state-pension-statement for state pension statement telling you how much you are likely to receive and when

Chapter 4

Set Realistic Goals

Goals need to inspire you. They will do this if they are realistic; otherwise they will hinder you.

We are going to identify which, if any, of your goals are unrealistic using the methodology I have developed. If you allow yourself to run too far with those hopes without applying any kind of stress testing, at some point the realisation that they may be unachievable becomes de-motivational, which is something to be avoided altogether.

For example, if you have the goal of retiring within the next six months on an income of £100k per annum and the only savings you have access to are a pension fund worth £500k, it's obviously not going to work because the pension fund just can't generate the level of income you're looking for and it will likely cause you to give up the idea altogether.

But if you slightly adjust your goal you might then say to yourself:

Within the next five years, I'm going to retire on £100k per annum. I'm going to achieve this by downsizing my property, maximising my pension contributions by paying in as much as I can over the next five years and then working part-time, say, two or three days a week, whatever's necessary to bridge the gap.

It may sound like a compromise, but it makes the goal more *realistic* and *believable* and *something which can be achieved*.

SMART goal setting

Now that you've begun to consider what your goals might be, the next step is to make sure they are SMART. Rather than being simply a vaguely defined wish list of dreams, SMART goal setting enables you to create a trackable path towards each goal objective, with clear timelines and an estimation of the goal's attainability. Every goal or objective can be made SMART and as such, brought closer to reality by applying these simple principles. A SMART goal should be:

S - specific
M - measurable
A - attainable
R - relevant
T - time-sensitive

Specific. A specific goal has a much greater chance of being accomplished than a general goal.

A non-specific goal might be 'I want to lose weight'. A specific goal would be 'I want to lose 28 pounds by 31 December this year.'

Measurable. To determine if your goal is measurable, ask questions such as: 'How much? How many? How will I know when it is accomplished?' Therefore, establish concrete criteria for measuring progress toward the attainment of each goal you set.

A non-measureable goal is to say 'I'll get fit'. A measureable goal is to say 'I will have a £1 million pension fund by age 65'.

Attainable. Dream big and aim for the stars, but keep one foot firmly based in reality. You can attain almost any goal you set when you plan wisely and establish a time frame that allows you to carry out those steps. However, resist the urge to set goals that are too easy or fanciful. By setting realistic yet challenging goals, you achieve the balance you need.

A non-attainable goal would be winning the London Marathon if you are aged over 50. An attainable goal might be to train hard and finish first in your age category in the London Marathon.

Relevant. To be relevant, a goal must represent an objective towards which you are both *willing* and *able* to work. There's no point setting a series of goals because you think it's going to make other people happy. Consider what is truly important to you and your life and if the goals you have set don't resonate with you, then it's time to reconsider them and look at them again.

A relevant goal would be to double your business profits so you can afford to buy your dream house and live in a much nicer area. A non-relevant goal would be to double your businesses profits because you think it will improve your failing marriage.

Time-sensitive. You only react with the appropriate energy and urgency if you have a clearly-defined timeframe for the goal; with no time frame linked to it there's no sense of urgency. If you want to lose 10lbs, when do you want to lose it by? 'Someday' simply won't work. But if you anchor it within a timeframe 'By May 1', then you've set your unconscious mind into motion to begin working on the goal. Additional ways to know if your goal is realistic is to determine if you have accomplished anything similar in the past or ask yourself what conditions would have to exist to accomplish this goal.

Case Study

Business owner Frank Dealy had an unrealistic goal. He was keen to retire and dreamt of buying a yacht and pursuing his dream of spending six months a year sailing. He wanted to sell his business and his accountant valued it at £5m and advised him not to sell for a penny less. But the business owner had received an offer for £4m. Looking at his financial plan, he could do absolutely everything he wanted to do in his life for far less than the £4m offered, but the accountant persuaded him to turn it down.

Unfortunately, he received no further offers and six months later he had lost all passion for the business and wanted out. The more he thought about it the more he realised it really didn't matter to him about getting the 'fair' market price arrived at by his accountant. The accountant was looking at it from a purely financial perspective and had not considered the business owner's real goal. He then decided he should go back and accept the original £4m offer, except now the buyer, sensing that he was desperate to sell, offered him considerably less. Because the business owner had procrastinated and was distracted by single-minded advice, not only did he lose six months of enjoying a better quality of life, he also lost an awful lot of money in the business that had become devalued in the eyes of the buyer, due to the owner's desperation.

This demonstrates that it's vital to know what your goal really is. You should ask yourself 'what am I really trying to achieve?'

Case Study

Katherine O'Brien, a 55-year-old client, was more realistic. She sought my advice since she was seriously contemplating early retirement. She'd long since stopped enjoying her work as a senior business analyst and although she was well paid, was still working extremely long hours and felt immensely stressed, not enjoying life at all. She had little time to enjoy her main passions, which were golf and travel.

Due to various cutbacks, her employers were throwing more and more work at her as well and expecting her to meet tight deadlines. But she had recently received an inheritance from her father and also built up some worthwhile pension benefits in the 30-odd years she'd been at work. The death of her father, plus the fact that a good golfing buddy had recently suffered a stroke, brought Katherine to the realisation that the life she was hoping to live when she retired might never happen if she didn't do something about it soon. She doubted she would be able to afford to retire early and had always assumed that 60 would be the earliest age she could realistically consider.

Using all the information Katherine provided, I prepared a lifelong cashflow forecast which included all of her anticipated outgoings in retirement, plus a reasonable allowance for her to pursue her main two hobbies of golf and travel, but it was falling a bit short of becoming achievable. Her goals and expectations were only slightly unrealistic and we therefore only needed to tweak them a little. With some careful tax planning and restructuring of her pension plan and investments, which took full advantage of the available tax breaks, I was able to create a plan which enabled Katherine to retire straight away.

The key change that made it possible for her to retire was the way in which she managed her father's inheritance. Up until this point, this money had lain dormant in a savings account, earning very little interest. But by reinvesting that money into a portfolio which, although more growth-orientated, still closely matched her risk profile, she was able to achieve her goal.

The portfolio we put together for Katherine was also significantly more tax efficient than the savings account. She was able to maximise her Individual Savings Account (ISA) allowance and further benefitted by utilising her annual capital gains tax-exempt allowance wherever possible. Katherine knows she won't make gains every single year; some years she will have losses, but most years, as long as the portfolio is gaining in value she will draw down gains and treat them as a tax-free income. The income from her ISAs is tax-free as well. She put the rest of her money into some insurance bonds which allow her to withdraw up to 5% per annum and this is tax-deferred for 20 years.

Rearranging Katherine's affairs in this way was what made the difference between retiring at 55 instead of 60 and living the life she dreamt of five years earlier! No wonder she immediately handed in her notice and after three months began living her dream life.

Now complete the form following the SMART principles and take your first steps towards making your goals something concrete to aim for.

SMART Goal-Setting

In a note book or on a piece of paper, write down your goals in as few words as possible

Make your goal SPECIFIC

How will you reach this goal? List at least three action steps you'll take (be specific):

1. _____

2. _____

3. _____

Make your goal MEASURABLE

I will measure/track my goal by using the following numbers or methods:
I will know I've reached my goal when:

1. _____

2. _____

3. _____

Make your goal ATTAINABLE

What additional resources do you need for success?

Items I need to achieve this goal:

How I'll find the time:

Things I need to learn more about:

People I can talk to for support:

Make your goal RELEVANT

List why you want to reach this goal:

1. _____

2. _____

3. _____

Make your goal TIME-SENSITIVE

I will reach my goal by (date):

My halfway measurement will be _____ on (date): _____

Additional dates and milestones I'll aim for:

1. _____

2. _____

3. _____

Chapter 5

Develop A Written Action Plan

'If you fail to plan, you are planning to fail!'
Benjamin Franklin

Congratulations! You have now reached the stage where you have completed the Vision Discovery process and selected some achievable goals. But you now need a plan in order to be able to achieve them. This chapter sets out the steps you will need to take in order to create your plan. This is the point where you will start to identify the appropriate investment, savings and protection solutions you will need to achieve the plan.

Committing to a written plan for your financial future is one of the most important things you can do. It's all very well having ideas in your head, but you need to write them down in order to make sure your plan happens. This will also strengthen your commitment to your plan. It's a bit like when you make a declaration and sign it, you feel more committed and from that point forward it takes on a reality that is harder to ignore or forget. You also need a plan to refer to over and over again, so that you can see what you were originally aiming for, since you will need to review it every year. Without having a written plan to refer to, it's difficult to see what you were aiming at in the first place. Think of this part of the process as if you were writing a letter of intent to yourself and signing a contract for your future financial benefit.

In this chapter I am going to explain to you the three steps you need to follow in order to create your plan, plus I will also provide details of how you can access the risk profiling tool I use in my practice. It's called FinaMetrica and readers of this book are entitled to a complimentary risk profile report. This will give you an understanding of the level of risk you are comfortable with when making investments. I can't overstress the importance of understanding your attitude to risk and I strongly recommend you take advantage of this tool as part of the process of creating your financial plan.

Capacity for Loss and your Attitude to Risk

Although I will guide you through these terms in more detail below, it's worth pausing for thought if you are currently in a position where your money is tied up in investments and you are about to set yourself some goals based on how well these might perform. For example, if your main goal is to retire at 60 and you've factored in all the assumptions into your future financial plan that I will set out in the next chapter, ask yourself, how would your plan be affected if 2008 and the great financial crash were to happen all over again? What would be your capacity for loss? This is a term given to the amount you could afford to lose on your retirement investments or capital. What is your attitude to risk? Are you the type of person who thinks that the more risk you're prepared to take, the higher the potential returns could be? The downside is that any losses are potentially greater. Whilst your attitude to risk may not change, due to life's circumstances, your capacity for loss does, so it's important to review this every year and to factor this into your plan. If you are desperate to retire at 60, ask yourself, can you deal with the fact that your portfolio or your investments are going to be up and down like a yo-yo in order to get you that higher return that you're seeking? Or if you don't want to change your risk profile, can you afford to save more? You will know from your cash flow whether you've got disposable income and whether it's possible to save more money. At the end of this book is a website link to some free-to-use financial planning software which will point you in the right direction. For example, it might show that by just saving an extra £250 a month now you could achieve your goal at 60 without the need to take any more risk or downsize your property.

Step 1 - Identify your Risk Profile

Risk profiling is a process for finding the optimal level of investment risk you are willing to accept because you need to understand the level of risk you are prepared to take with any investments that you make. To do this you will need to establish your level of risk tolerance before you begin choosing investments as part of your plan by considering the following points and asking these questions:

1. Risk Required - what is the risk associated with the return required to achieve your goals from the financial resources you have available?

2. Risk Capacity/Capacity for Loss - what is the level of financial risk that you can afford to take?

3. Risk Tolerance - what is the level of risk you are comfortable with?

Risk Required (1) and Risk Capacity (2) are financial characteristics which can be calculated using specialist financial planning software (shown in Chapter 3) where you generate your lifelong cashflow forecast. Risk Tolerance (3) is a psychological characteristic which is assessed separately using risk profiling software.

Both Risk Capacity and Risk Tolerance act separately as constraints on what you might otherwise do to achieve your goals. If, during this process, you discover a mismatch between Risk Required, Risk Capacity and Risk Tolerance, you must make trade-off decisions in order to reach the best possible solution.

What is Risk?

There is no one definition of the term Risk and everyone will have their own individual response to it. For
some it provides a thrill, no matter what the outcome;
to others, it means opportunity or uncertainty. However,
whenever there is the chance of multiple outcomes from
any given situation, this involves some level of risk to
a higher or lower degree. Each person will regard risk
differently and whilst some will never be tempted to
take any type of risk at all, others will embrace risk with
open arms. Risk tolerance is the level of risk a person
prefers to take.

When it comes to taking financial risks, a low risk tolerance can prevent many people from doing as well as they
could financially, whereas there are dangers in over-expos-
ing yourself to risk (and potential financial losses) if you go
beyond your own level of comfort (i.e. exceeding your risk
tolerance). It's therefore natural that many people are more
risk-avoiding that risk-taking in financial matters - but this
may also result in missed opportunities. It's about trying to
establish the right balance that is comfortable for you.

Understanding Risk Tolerance

Risk Tolerance is the extent to which you as an investor are comfortable with the risk of losing money on an investment. If you're unwilling to take the chance that an investment might drop in price, you have little or no risk tolerance. On the other hand, if you're willing to take some risk by making investments that fluctuate in value, you have greater risk tolerance. The probable consequence of limiting investment risk is that you are vulnerable to inflation risk, or loss of buying power. Risk tolerance changes with age, income and financial goals and is a psychological trait which naturally varies from person to person. Typically it decreases slowly with age and, as with other aspects of personality, may be altered by major life events, good or bad. Risk tolerance, as with other aspects of personality, is determined by genetics and life experiences. Essentially, it is settled by early adulthood. Accordingly, I recommend your risk tolerance should be retested every two or three years and also after any major life event.

Step 2 - Create your own Risk Profile Report

I recommend using a risk profiling tool called FinaMetrica. This is the same tool I use in my financial planning practice and whilst there are number of others available online, I have found FinaMetrica to be the most accurate. The system provides a scientific assessment of your personal financial risk tolerance and is used by leading advisers in 23 countries. Readers of this book have complimentary access to this software (normally only available for clients of my firm). For your access code please send an email to:

info@turbin.co.uk

entering in the subject line 'ONE DAY IS NOW FinaMetrica'

You can then begin to complete the questionnaire (note, your privacy and data is securely protected and will not be shared with anyone). There are two surveys to choose from: the 25-question version is appropriate if you are creating a comprehensive financial plan that deals with pretty much everything. Or if you have only identified one specific goal to which you have allocated a specific amount of money you may wish to use the shorter, 12-question version

Whichever version you choose, you will receive your own risk profile report which will provide you with your risk score and the risk group you fit into. You will then be able to download and save a PDF file of the report generated for you based on your responses.

FinaMetrica is one of a number of systems that provides a comprehensive assessment of your personal financial risk tolerance through an in-depth, but easy to complete, online survey that has been designed scientifically and thoroughly tested. Before the availability of such systems risk profiling was far more basic and completely inadequate. Most Financial Advisers would ask their clients just three basic questions:

Are you:

- Cautious?
- Balanced?
- Adventurous?'

The answers to these questions on their own and without expansion, only provide a sparse amount of information about an investor's attitude to risk and are open to the interpretation of the Financial Adviser. It is clear to see why there have been so many misunderstandings in the past between clients and their advisers who relied only on the answers to these three questions, sometimes without even defining what cautious, balanced or adventurous meant to them!

If you decide not to use the FinaMetrica software, opting for a meeting with a Financial Adviser instead, be aware that were you to be asked these three questions only, you must ensure that you or they define what is actually meant by, for example,' cautious', because it may be a completely different definition from the one you have in your head. You basically need to know you're both singing from the same hymn sheet. Otherwise, this three-question formula is simply not scientific enough - it can lead to unhealthy disagreements about what the appropriate level of risk should actually have been, after a dramatic downturn such as the one experienced in 2008.

By completing the more in-depth 25-question FinaMetrica profile, with its carefully-selected questions, there is less opportunity for misinterpretation and you will understand yourself better than the vast majority of people in similar situations who haven't gone through this process. You will be more confident as a result of the plan you decide to implement, based on your personality and circumstances.

Interpreting your Risk Report

Your Personal Financial Risk Tolerance Report will be prepared from information you provide, and is, therefore, only relevant to you. If, for example, you are one of a couple who make joint decisions, your partner should also take a risk tolerance test. Both sets of test results then need to be considered.

Your Personal Financial Risk Tolerance Report compares your answers to those given by a very large sample of the adult population. If you use a Financial Adviser in preparing this report, make sure that you discuss all of the results and especially any area that is seen to deviate from normal expectations, based on your profile. Remember to take notes during this meeting and to agree between you that the notes are a true and accurate record of the meeting in order to avoid any future misunderstandings.

Once you have generated your Personal Financial Risk Tolerance Report it will assist you in your financial decision-making but the report or FinaMetrica itself will not endorse or suggest any course of action you decide to take, based on the report. Those decisions are for you and/or your Financial Adviser to agree.

Step 3 - Asset Allocation

Having completed the report you now know what your risk profile tells you about yourself and you need to determine how to best allocate your money between the various different asset classes available for you to invest in e.g. equities, bonds and short-term reserves, cash, etc. This spread of different types of asset classes is your asset allocation.

I cannot over-emphasise the importance of asset allocation. Therefore, you need to ensure you create a suitable asset allocation for your investment portfolio. This stage of the financial planning process is critical and is without doubt the number one factor in determining the long-term performance of portfolios. It is also the single most important factor in managing the volatility of your portfolio. In Nick Murray's book *Behavioral Investment Counseling* he refers to a well-known 1986 report entitled *Determinants of Portfolio Performance*. Authors of the report Gary Brinson, L. Randolph Hood and Gilbert Beebower concluded that asset allocation accounted for 93% of variance in return and volatility. This means that only 7% came from other factors such as fund selection.

When creating your asset allocation bear in mind that over the long-term portfolios that hold the highest proportion of equities have performed best. However I'm talking about the serious long term here and in the short term equities can be highly volatile so if your goal is 10 years or less away a high allocation to equities could be risky and result in you falling short of your target.

To emphasise the inflation-busting quality of equities Murray gives another example in his book which shows the return of different asset classes over the 81 years from 1926 to 2007. Equities delivered an after inflation return of just over 7% whereas bonds provided a little over 2%. In other words equities delivered a return more than three times greater than that of bonds.

You should not select investments until you've decided on the right asset allocation for you . Remember, riskier investments such as equities should provide the best returns over the longer term but are also likely to be the most volatile, so investing in a combination of different types of asset can help reduce the severity of those swings in value, particularly if they're non-correlated, i.e. their prices move independently. Non-correlated assets might be equities and bonds for example. They are not correlated, so when the stock market is going through a particularly volatile period, your bonds won't necessarily be experiencing volatility at the same time. Therefore, it usually makes sense for investors who are looking for growth, as opposed to income, to hold a mixture of equities, bonds and cash even though the long-term growth potential of these other asset classes is less than if you hold equities alone. This way, you can control the volatility to a certain extent, so the asset allocation has a direct impact on the level of risk in your investment portfolio.

Now you can see why your FinaMetrica risk profile is so important. It will help you gauge how much equity you are comfortable with in your portfolio. If, for example you are fairly cautious and any fall of, say 10% or so, would make you uncomfortable you are highly unlikely to stick with an asset allocation that has 100% in equities. You don't want to be in the position where you are spilling your morning coffee down your favourite shirt in alarm as you check online and see your portfolio is down 40%! Yes we know that it will recover in time (history proves this) but the key is not to get outside your own comfort zone. Otherwise you will become an average, or worse, losing investor by reacting to events and cashing in your portfolio at the worst possible time (more on this later).

It is also vital you don't take your eyes off your ultimate goal. For example if you can achieve your goal of retiring at 60 with an average annual return of 5% and this is possible with only a small exposure to equities then why go for more? Your asset allocation needs to match your risk profile and goals.

I hope now you are beginning to see how this all interacts. That is why I started by talking about your goals before going on to discuss your risk profile and then asset allocation.

Another important factor to take account of is the timescale of your goals when selecting your asset allocation.

For example, if your goal is five years away, you should probably take much less risk than if it were 20 years away and this will inevitably affect your asset allocation, i.e. how much you intend to allocate to equities versus bonds and cash, thus, you're going to put less into equities.

For a comprehensive resource in helping you choose your asset allocation I highly recommend Richard Ferri's excellent book *All About Asset Allocation*. In addition I have provided links to popular online tools at the end of this chapter which should provide some help in determining your ideal asset allocation for each of your goals.

Links

Asset Allocation

www.vanguard.co.uk/uk/portal/investor-resources/learning/tools
basic free asset allocation tool

www.morningstar.co.uk
more sophisticated asset allocation tool, subscription fee of £159 per annum (as of July 2015)

Chapter 6

Implement Your Plan

Very soon it will be time to choose the investment vehicles you intend to use to achieve your financial plan but first here's a summary of where we are so far:

You should now have a clear idea of your goals and an understanding of the level of risk you are willing to take in order to achieve them. You have also created an appropriate asset allocation for each one of you goals.

Congratulations, you have a plan!

Now it's time for you to put that plan into action. What once may have seemed like a grey and foggy subject matter you've been putting off for that one day in the future, should now be much clearer for you to see . Following the 6-step process in this book will dramatically increase the likelihood of you accomplishing your goals. So far you should have:

- Created your lifelong cash flow forecast which incorporates details of your present and anticipated future income including: your state pension forecast; any private pension income; income from investment property or part-time work etc.).

- Prepared your net worth statement summarising your current assets including: all your existing investment holdings; pension funds and any property or business assets owned.
  Included in your cash flow forecast details of any anticipated future lump sums you are likely to receive, for example: inheritances; your current expenses and planned future expenses (including any large one-offs as a result of your goal-setting session, e.g., daughter's wedding, world cruise. Include details of any debts, e.g. mortgage, and the date by which they are going to be extinguished.

Check – you will have determined that your plan is realistic and achievable having taken into account your risk profile and you will have decided upon a suitable asset allocation for your investments.

Check – you will have also stress-tested your plan to make sure it can cope with various catastrophes, for example, a stock market crash, if you were to suffer a critical illness or die prematurely or if you were to need long-term care in later life and identified any weaknesses.

Check – if you have completed all of the above, then you have arrived at the point where you are almost ready to implement your plan.

Choose appropriate financial products (Choosing your Investments)

For a Financial Adviser to provide investment advice it is imperative they have a complete understanding of their client's specific circumstances. Therefore it's not possible in a book such as this to offer any specific advice on which investments you should select for your portfolio.

However, I can say that another important decision you need to make is the type of 'wrappers' in which you are going to choose to hold your investments. Wrapper selection will determine the tax treatment of your investments so it's important to know the benefits and disadvantages of each of the main tax wrappers available in the United Kingdom and how they relate to your own tax status. Selecting the right wrappers should help to minimise the tax that you pay on the returns that your money and investments earn and therefore, all other things being equal, increase the speed at which you achieve you goals.

There now follows a short description of some of the most popular financial products available in the UK. It is not intended to be a comprehensive guide but should prove helpful in your quest to select suitable investment and protection solutions for your plan.

Protection (insurance) against catastrophic events

If critical illness or life insurance is not an employee benefit offered to you (or you are self-employed without similar cover) then I strongly recommend you choose the appropriate financial product to meet your needs. Even if you *are* covered by your employer, or if you are self-employed and currently without any cover, it is still important to calculate if you need to top up the insured sum in order for your plan to work.

If you have identified weaknesses that can be insured against you should consider putting in place one or more of the policy types shown below to protect you and your family. For example, if you are 55 and your plan shows you paying off your mortgage by 65, what would happen if you were to die prematurely or suffer a debilitating critical illness before you retired?

Your plan will fail.

Life Insurance and Critical Illness Insurance are products specifically designed to protect you/your family by covering such eventualities. Both types of insurance pay out a predetermined tax-free lump sum when such an emergency or life-changing event occurs. But if you are an employee, before you run headlong into researching these insurance policies, it's important to find out what benefits your employer currently includes as part of your remuneration package. Many employers provide insurance that would pay up to four times your salary as a death-in-service benefit and some even provide critical illness cover too. Once you know what your employer provides it's fairly easy to calculate any shortfall in these arrangements. For example, if your current salary is £50,000 per year and your employer offers four times salary death in service benefit this will equate to £200,000. If your outstanding mortgage is £300,000, you have a shortfall of £100,000 and should probably consider purchasing a further £100,000 worth of cover (assuming one of your goals is to pay off your mortgage completely in the event that you die).

Life Insurance

This provides a cash lump sum in the event of your death. Typically you pay a monthly premium to your insurer for the insurance which protects your loved ones from financial hardship if you die prematurely. The lump sum can be used then to help pay off a mortgage, debts, your family's day-to-day expenses and even help towards funeral costs.

Income replacement (also known as Permanent Health Insurance)

These policies help replace your earned income if you are unable to work as a result of long-term illness or disability. Usually there is a deferred period of three to six months before the policy would pay out so short term illness-es would not be covered. The general rule is that shorter deferred periods give rise to higher insurance premiums which stands to reason as the risk to the insurers of having to pay out increases.

Critical Illness Insurance

Critical illness insurance policies provide financial protection in the event you suffer a critical illness. Policies pay out a predetermined lump sum once the illness has been diagnosed. Not all insurers cover the same illnesses so it's important to ask your insurer for a full list of the illnesses covered. Practically all policies do however cover the big three of cancer, heart attack and stroke as standard.

Examples of other conditions that might be covered include:

- Alzheimer's disease
- blindness
- deafness
- kidney failure
- a major organ transplant
- multiple sclerosis
- HIV/AIDS contracted by blood transfusion or during an operation
- Parkinson's disease

- paralysis of limb
- terminal illness

You can compare life, critical illness and income protection policies at websites such as www.comparethemarket.com or www.moneysupermarket.com

Select suitable savings accounts and investments

Savings

If protection could be considered the cornerstone of your financial plan then certainly the foundation should be your cash reserves. It is essential before you make any other investments to set aside adequate funds to allow for emergencies and other unforeseen events. Your cash reserve is a pool of, money you can easily get your hands on if your roof suddenly caves in! Having this reserve prevents you having to make costly investing mistakes such as being forced into selling equities (which we have already agreed should only ever be considered a long-term investment) in order to meet short-term challenges. Your plan will be far less effective if you invest everything you have into stocks and shares as there is a very real possibility of you losing money should you be forced to access these investments in the early years of your plan.

Whilst money left on deposit is not really an investment at all and has failed to keep pace with inflation over the longer term, you should try and keep this 'comfort money' to a sensible amount by only maintaining your emergency funds in cash.

Tip 1: *Don't keep more than you need to on deposit because anything more than that means your money isn't working for you. Over the long-term cash deposits have failed to keep pace with inflation and whilst UK interest rates remain at record lows any money left on deposit is likely to be losing value in real terms.*

Over the years many people have asked me what is the optimum amount of cash to hold in reserve? I tell them what I tell all of my clients, which is that there is no definitive right amount and that each person is different. However as a suggestion you should consider maintaining between three to six months' expenses in a deposit account in order to provide for emergencies. If however you are going to feel very uncomfortable with this I suggest you up it to 12 months' expenses. That shouldn't be enough for inflation to do any real harm to your future prosperity. Any amount more than this is, in my opinion, a poor use of money.

Tip 2: *Only keep around 20% of your cash reserve on instant access. The remainder should be placed in a higher-rate deposit account where you might have to give 30 days' notice or lose interest to access sooner. Even though this might mean you forgo the interest if you withdraw without notice, it is unlikely you will ever need the money in less than 30 days and you will earn a little more interest whilst on deposit.*

You should research the best interest rate achievable by placing the majority of your cash on term deposit. This type of account generally pays more interest because it typically requires you to give notice of 30 or 90 days to access your cash or you suffer a penalty (usually a loss of some, or all, of the interest). The remainder would probably best be placed on instant access to cover immediate unforeseen expenses. You can often get a better rate of interest in an ISA savings account (more about ISA's later) but if you use up your annual ISA allowance in this way you will not be able to use it to hold stocks and shares. Do your research first using sites such as www.gocompare.com or www.moneysupermarket.com and select accounts most suited to your requirements.

Tip 3: *If you still intend to hold a more significant sum on deposit of over £85,000 (as of the time of writing) remember that in the event of the financial institution failing (as could happen and nearly did with Northern Rock in 2007) you will be only guaranteed to recover £85,000 from the Financial Services Compensation Scheme (FSCS) even if you hold, for example £200,000 spread over a number of accounts with the same bank. The guarantee applies per customer and not per the number of accounts that you hold with that particular bank. Therefore its best to spread your investment between different financial institutions so that you don't hold more than £85,000 with any single one. Also be aware the maximum compensation figure will drop to £75,000 with effect from 1 January 2016.*

Investments

There are almost an infinite number of investment possibilities available for you to use in your financial planning and it is not my intention to provide an exhaustive list of them in this book. However, I believe it will now be useful to provide a summary of some of the most popular investment types and those which I most often use when advising my financial planning clients:

New Individual Savings Accounts (NISAs)

A NISA is available to any UK resident over the age of 18. NISAs offer a number of tax advantages. You do not have to pay any income or capital gains tax on investment returns, and no tax is payable on money withdrawn. It is possible to hold cash and a broad range of other investments such as stocks and shares or bonds within the arrangement, and there are no restrictions on when or how much money can be withdrawn. Although it differs from a pension in that there is no tax relief on contributions going in it can be a useful way to boost retirement savings in support of your pension arrangements. As of the 2015/16 tax year it is possible to subscribe up to £15,240 per person to a NISA. This limit is normally increased in the budget each year.

Alternative Investment Market (AIM) NISA

Although I recommend ISA's a lot to clients in my practice I have found that as clients age and start to focus more on reducing their Inheritance Tax (IHT) burden traditional ISAs become a less appropriate investment. This is because they form part of your taxable estate on death.

In August 2013 when the government changed the ISA rules and allowed AIM shares to be held by and ISA for the first time I became excited by the possibilities for reducing IHT for clients.

For those investors with a suitable attitude to risk (AIM ISAs are higher risk and offer less liquidity than standard stock and shares ISAs) this represented a significant planning opportunity.

This is because certain AIM shares held in an ISA qualify for Business Property Relief and are exempt from Inheritance Tax once they have been held for two years and they still offer all the existing tax advantages of a traditional ISA. This is not the case with most ordinary stocks and shares or cash ISAs.

Make no mistake, AIM ISAs are likely to be more volatile than traditional ISAs but if your risk profile allows it – and perhaps you already hold a diverse portfolio of other assets - then investing in an AIM ISA is well worth considering. If you've not already considered doing so, it could be worth your while transferring funds from your existing ISAs into an AIM ISA since the existing ISAs form part of your estate (and are therefore, potentially subject to Inheritance Tax).

It is impossible for me to comment here whether an AIM ISA is an appropriate investment for you so if you are in any doubt please consult a suitably qualified Financial Planner.

Junior Individual Savings Accounts (JISAs)

Junior ISAs were introduced in November 2011 and offer the same tax benefits as adult ISA's. The maximum allowable subscription for 2015/16 tax year is £4,080. They are available to children under the age of 18 at which time the JISA converts to an adult ISA. As with adult ISAs, JISAs can invest in both cash and stocks and shares. Funds may not be withdrawn until the child reaches 18 unless a terminal illness claim is agreed or following closure of the account after the death of the child. A child can open their own account from 16, otherwise a person with parental responsibility must do it.

For more information, visit

https://www.gov.uk/junior-individual-savings-accounts/overview

National Savings and Investments

There is a wide range of investments offered by the UK government a full list of which is available at www.nsandi.com.

Investment Bonds

Investment bonds are a type of life insurance policy into which you can invest a lump sum. There are a variety of different fund choices available to invest in via an investment bond. You will have a choice of two types of funds into which your bond can invest – with-profits or unit-linked. Both types of fund have the same tax treatment in that tax is paid on both growth and income accrued in the fund by the insurer. They're not to be confused with corporate bonds, premium bonds or fixed-rate bonds since they are actually a type of investment fund.

Minimum investment levels will vary from one insurer to the next but typically will range between £5,000 and £10,000 and most investment bonds are whole of life policies. There is no minimum term, usually, although surrender penalties may apply in the early years.

The policyholder does not receive income from the policy (although it is possible to make withdrawals) so personal income tax is deferred until certain events occur and the insurance company calculates any gain on a bond. As a result, an investment bond is a potentially tax-efficient way of holding a range of investment funds in one place.

Collective Investment Schemes (Unit Trusts and Open Ended Investment Companies (OEICS), Exchange Traded Funds (ETFs)

Collective investment schemes are funds which give investors access to a wide variety of different asset classes such as equities, bonds, commodities and property. Investing in collectives gives individual investors the opportunity to achieve a diverse spread of these assets with a relatively small amount of capital and this in turn spreads risk. For example a typical US equity OEIC could often hold around 100 separate equities and investors could access such a fund for only a £1,000 minimum investment. It simply wouldn't be possible to purchase this many equities individually with £1,000.

Venture Capital Trusts (VCTs)

A VCT is a company whose shares trade on the London stock market that aims to make money by investing in other companies. These are typically very small companies which are looking for further investment to help develop their business. VCTs are considered higher risk investments and whilst they attract some very significant tax advantages, it's important to note that they will really only appeal to an investor with a suitably high-risk profile. Therefore, you need to be sure that any investment into a VCT fits with the risk profile you've already created and that you're not investing just for a tax break.

Tax advantages offered by VCTs:

- up to 30% income tax relief on investments up to £200,000 in any tax year (to retain this relief you have to hold the VCT shares for at least five years).
- tax-free dividends.
- no capital gains tax.

Income Tax relief is provided as a tax credit to set against your total income tax liability and, therefore, cannot exceed your total tax liability for the tax year. You won't get this tax relief if you buy existing Venture Capital Trust shares.

Enterprise Investment Scheme (EIS)

Similar to a venture capital trust except these are intended to be held for a minimum of three years. Like VCTs, EISs are a higher risk investment that offer an even greater number of tax advantages.

The EIS is designed to help smaller higher-risk trading companies to raise finance by offering a range of tax reliefs to investors who purchase new shares in those companies. Tax relief is available to individuals only, who subscribe for (although this can be through a nominee), shares in an EIS. Relief is at 30% of the cost of the shares, to be set against the individual's Income Tax liability for the tax year in which the investment was made.

Tax advantages of EISs

- Investors can claim income tax relief on up to 30% of the value of an EIS investment (up to a maximum of £1 million invested in each tax year).

- Investors facing capital gains tax liabilities on other investments can use an EIS investment to defer the capital gain. Tax won't be due for as long as their EIS investment is held and the capital gain will be eliminated if the EIS shares are held at death.

- EIS investments are expected to become 100% inheritance tax exempt after they are held for two years, as long as the investor still owns the EIS shares when they die.

- Investors won't be required to pay any tax on gains made from the sale of their EIS shares.

- Investors can apply for up to 45% loss relief on any holding within their EIS portfolio that is sold at a loss.

Personal Pensions and Self-Invested Personal Pensions (SIPPs)

Personal Pensions

A personal pension is a type of defined contribution scheme and is an excellent way to save for retirement. This is because investors receive a number of attractive tax incentives for investing in a personal pension and so such investments (setting the issue of fund performance to one side) grow faster than other types of investment which don't benefit from these tax breaks.

You choose the provider and make arrangements for your contributions to be paid. Often, these types of pensions are provided by insurance companies who will more than likely ask you to choose from one of their in-house funds. However, low charges and a favourable contract doesn't always mean the fund will perform well but certainly, if you haven't got a workplace pension, getting a personal pension could be a good way of saving for retirement. Whichever pension provider you choose, it will claim tax relief at the basic rate and add it to your pension pot. If you're a higher rate taxpayer then you will need to claim the additional rebate through your tax return.

SIPPs

A SIPP or Self Invested Personal Pension is essentially just a more sophisticated version of a personal pension. The main difference is that it offers you a much wider choice of investment possibilities and you can choose and manage the investments made yourself if you so wish. SIPPs are designed for people who want to manage their own funds by dealing with, and switching, their investments when they want to. SIPPs can also have higher charges than other personal pensions or stakeholder pensions. For these reasons, SIPPs tend to be more suitable for larger funds and for people who are experienced in investing.

Most common types of Investment that can be held in a SIPP

- Individual Shares
- Funds e.g. Unit Trusts
- Investment Trusts
- Exchange Traded Funds (ETFs)
- Government Bonds
- Commercial Property

Tax advantages of Personal Pensions and SIPPs

Tax relief

When you make a payment into your pension you receive tax relief from HM Revenue & Customs (HMRC). The effect of tax relief on pension payments over time can be considerable - the more you contribute, the more tax relief you can get, subject to the current HMRC limits outlined below.

Tax-efficient growth

Your pension fund grows largely tax-free, which can help to boost the amount you have in your fund.

Tax-free cash

You can usually take up to 25% of your pension savings tax free (depending on the your plan/scheme rules). The remainder of your pension will be taxed.

Current limits to how much tax relief you can get

You can get tax relief on every penny you contribute, up to 100% of your annual earnings, with an upper limit of £40,000 in 2015/16. This was reduced from £50,000 in the 2014/15 tax year.

It is also possible to carry forward any unused allowance from the previous three tax years 2012/13, 2013/14 and 2014/15 making it possible to contribute up to £180,000 in total in the current (2015/16) tax year (assuming no previous contributions were made).

If you don't pay tax, you can still benefit from tax relief on contributions you make, up to a limit of £2,880. The tax man will also add 20% to make the total £3,600.

As I mentioned earlier, this list of types of investments is not meant to be exhaustive but will give you a good insight into the most common types of investment vehicles currently available in the UK. You will need to determine which combination of these is most appropriate given your individual circumstances before deciding where to invest.

Product providers

Follow the web links in this book and carry out your own research into Life and Critical Illness Assurance, Income replacement Insurance, Savings Accounts and National Savings Products.

However, the world of investment products can be a maze and to the untrained eye of a would-be investor, the various terms, definitions and jargon can be difficult to negotiate on your own. With regards to which providers to choose for NISAs, AIM NISAs, Investment Bonds, VCTs, EISs, SIPPs and other investment products you may wish to engage the services of a suitably qualified financial planner. I recommend a Certified Financial Planner[cm] as they should follow the six- stage financial planning process I have outlined in this book as well as being able to recommend the most appropriate investments for you as an individual. You can find a list of CFP[cm] here: http://www.financialplanning.org.uk/wayfinder Alternatively you may contact me at info@turbin.co.uk and I will offer readers of this book a complimentary

30-minute consultation. It is, of course, possible to obtain advice from other institutions such as banks, but I would strongly caution against this. As in all walks of life, there are reputable and less reputable institutions to choose from, but again, it can be tricky choosing the right one for you. Whichever one you go for, bear in mind that a multi-national or global institution will also be looking to load its overhead costs on to your fees as well as trying to turn a profit. Some of these institutions are also trying to recover from near meltdown following the 2008 crash when they were bailed out at the taxpayers' (i.e. your) expense. They are also highly unlikely to offer true financial planning as described in this book or indeed truly independent financial advice.

Managing your investments using a platform

Depending on the size and number of your investments, if you hold them directly, managing them and switching funds from one to another can be time-consuming and complicated. You should therefore give serious consideration to holding them on a platform.

A platform is a service that allows you to hold and manage all your assets in one place. This service will save you a significant amount of hassle by releasing you from much of the time-consuming administration that is generally involved in managing your financial arrangements. In addition, you'll receive comprehensive statements and full documentation in respect of all purchases, sales, deposits and withdrawals. You will find that rebalancing your portfolio periodically is very straightforward and you'll also benefit from a single consolidated income tax report to help you or your accountant complete your tax return at the end of the financial year.

Another significant advantage is that you can obtain online valuations whenever you need them. This will save you valuable time as you can view all of your investments and their current values in an instant rather than having to contact lots of different companies to obtain this information.

Platform providers act in accordance with the rules set by the Financial Conduct Authority and your money is directly invested in the investment companies you choose and their funds. Platforms also allow you buy and sell investments simply and to restructure your Portfolio online, 24/7. The charges you pay for using a platform provider will depend on the amount of money you invest as well as the investments you choose.

The following two examples will give you an idea of some strategies I have used when creating financial plans for my clients

Example 1

Peter and Anna are a couple approaching retirement with £300,000 to invest (excluding cash reserves for emergency funds). We have already determined their risk profile and have decided to place 50% of their funds in equities and 50% in fixed interest securities as this represents a suitable asset allocation given their risk profile and current objectives. Currently in the 2015/16 tax year they can invest £15,240 each (£30,480 total) into ISAs and we decide to fully utilise this. We then invest the remaining £269,520 into a portfolio of funds such as those described earlier. In subsequent tax years we then transfer the maximum ISA allowance for both of them from the portfolio of funds into new ISAs thereby maximum funding their ISA allowance for the foreseeable future. After approximately 10 years of following this strategy we will have invested the entire £300,000 so the whole portfolio will benefit from the preferential tax treatment afforded to ISAs.

Example 2

Ernie and Jane are a retired married couple in their mid-60s who engaged us to construct a comprehensive financial plan. They have two adult children and a combined pension income of £40,000 per year. Their house is currently worth £700,000; they hold £300,000 in investments and have £100,000 in cash. Their risk profile is fairly cautious and they are unsure if their current investment portfolio reflects their goals:

Goals

- Never run out of money during their lifetime
- Be well organised financially
- Investments to mirror cautious risk profile
- Mitigate tax as far as possible
- Retain sufficient funds for long-term-care should need arise

Challenges

- They are unsure if their retirement funds will last a lifetime
- Their existing investments are disorganised and lack tax efficiency
- A large number of their investment funds are high risk and don't match their cautious risk profile
- The existing investments include a number of with-profit bonds which have performed very poorly.
- Their estate has a significant Inheritance Tax liability and they are failing to use their annual Capital Gains Tax exemptions.
- They are unsure how much long term care would cost and are worried they might need to sell their house.

What we did

- Prepared a lifetime cashflow forecast
- Reduced their cash deposits to £30k (roughly 12 months expenses)
- Sold the poorly-performing With Profits Bonds
- Invested £100k in a discounted gift trust

- Reinvested the remaining investments (ISAs and Shares) into a suitably cautious portfolio of funds
- Maximised their ISA allowances for the current tax year

The Results

They were relieved to see that the cashflow forecast showed they would never run out of money (using very modest growth assumptions for their investments).

By placing the investments on a wrap platform they became well organised with everything now held in a single place.

By maximising their ISA allowances and disposing of the insurance bonds they significantly improved the tax efficiency of their investments.

By reinvesting the cash and insurance bond monies into the recommended portfolio of funds they greatly improved their growth prospects and ensured the investments matched their risk profile much more closely.

They immediately reduced their Inheritance Tax liability by £20k by using the discounted gift trust (with the prospect of further reductions after three years).

The cashflow showed they could comfortably increase spending by £5k per year or, if they desired, give it away to their children/grandchildren. This would allow them to enjoy a better quality of life and further reduce their Inheritance liability by £2,000 per year.

They structured their investments to take advantage of their annual capital gains tax allowance as far as they possibly could resulting in a further tax saving of around £900 per year.

The cashflow showed that they could afford care costs for up to 6 years should either of them need care meaning they would not have to sell their house.

In summary, they now have a clear plan and complete peace of mind that all their goals can be achieved. They are enjoying their retirement more, spending more than they previously felt able to and truly embracing the concept of 'one day is now'. This is the power of a well-constructed financial plan.

Chapter 7

Monitor And Adjust As Needed

Congratulations! By now you will have created - and implemented - your financial/life plan. You are well on the way to achieving your goals and living the life of your dreams. We now come to what I consider to be the single most important element of any good financial plan – monitoring and reviewing to keep it on track.

Your plan will need regular course corrections much in the same way as an aeroplane is off course for most of its journey and the pilot makes minor adjustments along the way to ensure it arrives safely at its destination. Your plan will be slightly off course most of the time and without your/your adviser's regular intervention it is unlikely you will reach your goals. Therefore, on an annual basis you should revisit and review your plan.

Remember even a well-constructed financial plan will contain a large number of assumptions. Assumptions about future inflation, growth of your investments, tax rates, increases in house prices, your continued good health etc. The only thing I can tell you with complete confidence about the future is that your assumptions (however well-reasoned) will be wrong! Sometimes they won't be out by much but on other occasions they may be significantly wide of the mark. The point is no one can accurately predict the future – check out the Chancellor's annual inflation forecast in the budget if you doubt this – so your plan will need regular reviews to take account of what actually did transpire in the previous twelve months.

Significant events such as the large market downturn which occurred in 2008 can also have an impact on your plan. I prefer to factor these events in by assuming they will happen (they nearly always do) every 10 years or so. However it's virtually impossible to consistently and accurately predict when they will happen so this is yet another reason why you should regularly review your plan. If you don't choose to factor in such events this may cause you to have to make a fairly substantial revision to your plan i.e. you may now need to save substantially more or delay your retirement several years to take account of this.

Even a fairly small discrepancy in your assumptions vs actual events can over time cause a plan to fail. For example, it is highly unlikely that your inflation assumption is going to be significantly wrong over a 12-month period. Perhaps it will differ by a half a percentage point from the actual recorded inflation figure from one year to the next. But if you ignore these small deviations, the compound effect over time can have a major impact on the effectiveness of your plan. You will need to update your plan to take account of such variations.

It is also important to take into account that the conditions which pertain today were not those that existed ten years ago and are therefore most unlikely to be those that pertain ten years from now. Your financial plan is a long-term forecast and so basing your assumptions on inflation always remaining at today's low levels is not what I would recommend. For example, in my practice, clients are sometimes initially confused as to why I currently use an assumption of 3% interest on their deposit accounts. They often make comments like 'I wish I knew of an account that does pay 3%, mine only pays 1%. Are you sure that's realistic, Martin?'

Once I explain to them that what I'm actually doing is forecasting sometimes 30-40 years into the future they understand the logic in not assuming interest rates will forever be at record lows. It's far more meaningful to look at long-term historical averages so this is what I do. My advice is not to fall into the trap of making assumptions based upon what prevails in the present time.

Of course your assumptions could also have been too conservative so incorrect assumptions don't always mean the postponement of your goals. For example – if your investments have grown by more than your assumptions you may now be able to bring forward a goal such as that of retiring at 65.

To see the assumptions I am currently using in my plans, log onto www.turbinfp.co.uk/free-resources

From here you can download the assumptions which will be updated periodically.

Rebalancing your Investments

Another essential part of your annual plan review and a key to being successful with your investing is to regularly rebalance your portfolio. Back in Chapter 5 we discussed choosing the most suitable asset allocation, taking into account your risk profile and investment goals. Rebalancing is the process of periodically restoring your asset allocation to your original target asset allocation. Your portfolio will automatically get out of balance the moment after it is created. This is because over any given period some of your chosen investments will perform well while others may not. The value of your portfolio will change on a daily basis depending upon where we are in any particular economic cycle so the asset allocation you selected could look very different after just six months. This was the very reason you created a diverse portfolio with different asset classes in the first place. You didn't put your eggs in one basket by investing in one asset class only, because you knew this was too risky. Different asset classes will perform well at different stages of the economic cycle. The problem is, no one can tell you consistently when each asset class is going to have a purple patch so you hold a basket of different assets – remember? The investments that have performed well are now going to constitute a bigger slice of you portfolio and, conversely those that haven't performed will make up a lesser part.

It is therefore essential, assuming your goals haven't changed, to rebalance your portfolio and restore its original asset allocation. Otherwise you could end up carrying far too much risk. Rebalancing is therefore, primarily, used to control risk.

For example, let's say your original asset allocation is 50% equities and 50% percent bonds. If share prices rise for a few months, your equities may now make up 60% of the portfolio. This means you should now sell some equities and use this money to purchase more bonds in order to restore your 50/50 split. If you decide not to rebalance you now have a 60/40 equities/bonds split which does not match your risk tolerance.

By rebalancing in this way (I recommend every six months, setting these dates in advance as we do in my practice on January 17th and July 17th every year) you will automatically be selling high, i.e. selling the asset that has done well and buying low in favour of buying the asset that has performed poorly. This is highly counter-intuitive and it's what separates a successful investor from an average one. It is human nature to want to hold on to that which has performed best. I often have to remind clients of this as they say 'but I don't want to sell that holding, it's been the best of the lot' or 'I don't want to buy any more bonds, they've been terrible'.

You must guard against this instinct and remain disciplined if you want a successful investing experience. The value of rebalancing is perfectly illustrated by the 2008 stock market downturn.

Continuing the 50/50 equity/bond example from above - for the first eight months of the year you could have been purring with satisfaction at how well your equities were performing. You may well have been reluctant to rebalance at all and yet, by the end of that year, you would probably be asking yourself why you hadn't. Once the value of equities had plummeted, your 50/50 asset allocation could easily have been 30/70 in favour of bonds.

Imagine you had previously decided to rebalance every January. How would you have felt buying equities at that time to restore your asset allocation? The media were extremely negative: it was different this time (it always is apparently!). You may have held off the rebalance as a result and missed the very best buying opportunity some of us will see in our lifetime, as equity values soared and eventually rose above their September 2008 values.

This is why it is critical to remain disciplined and follow your plan to rebalance every six months (or annually if you prefer). Don't let your emotions control your investment behaviour. If you doubt you have the discipline to follow your plan religiously then I again recommend you consider engaging a Certified Financial Planner[cm] to manage your investments for you.

Why rebalance?

Rebalancing instils in you a key discipline for successful investing – it forces you to take profits from investments that have increased in value and put money in things that have merit but haven't gone up in value.

A word of caution – Capital Gains Tax (CGT)

Because rebalancing involves selling the parts of your portfolio that have done well in order to buy more of the parts that haven't done so well, the process can result in you creating a capital gain. This would apply to any assets which are not held in a CGT-exempt wrapper such as a NISA or SIPP.

Whilst it is good practice to use up your annual capital gains tax exemption (each individual has an annual exemption which is £11,100 for the 2015/16 tax year) any gains made over and above this exemption will suffer tax at 18% (for basic rate taxpayers) and 28% for 40%/45% taxpayers.

Budgets will change things

Every year, or sometimes twice a year, there will be a budget and you need to take into account the impact of any budget announcements on your plan.

For example, in September 2015 there was an additional summer budget at which, among other things, the Chancellor of the Exchequer made the following announcements:

- The creation of an extra Inheritance Tax (IHT) nil-rate band for homeowners, worth £175,000 for individuals and £350,000 for couples. This will likely have a positive impact on any homeowners planning to mitigate IHT.

- A reduction in the pension contribution allowance for those earning more than £150,000 which will progressively reduce at a rate of £1 for every £2 earned over £150,000. As a result anyone earning over £210,000 will have an annual allowance of just £10,000. This will almost certainly mean higher earners planning to fund retirement income through pensions will need to look for alternatives.

- From April 2016 the 10% tax credit on dividend income will be abolished and replaced with a £5,000 annual allowance. Basic rate taxpayers will pay 7.5% tax on any dividend income over this allowance. Higher rate taxpayers will pay 32.5%

and additional rate taxpayers 38.1%. This news is a significant blow to any business owners who currently pay themselves by a combination of dividend and salary.

The one thing I would want to impress upon you in this chapter is to emphasise why a plan has to be dynamic and this will allow you adapt to the inevitable changes that will occur year by year. Therefore, review your plan.

Chapter 8

Don't Be An Active Investor!

'Most institutional and individual investors will find the best way to own common stock is through an index fund that charges minimal fees. Those following this path are sure to beat the net results (after fees and expenses) delivered by the great majority of investment professionals'.

Warren Buffet

Before I get into the explanation of active and passive management styles I think it would be useful to reprint an excerpt from my firm's Investment Policy Statement which will give you, the reader, a clear understanding of where I am positioned in the debate.

Excerpt from Investment Policy Statement September 2014

Active vs Passive Investing

Investment styles are often categorised as either active or passive. An active investor can be described as one who makes decisions about holding one investment over anoth-er. An active investor believes it is possible to beat the mar-ket. Passive investors are willing to accept the market rate of return and usually enjoy paying smaller fees than active in-vestors. A passive investor believes it is neither possible nor necessary to consistently beat the market to achieve their investment goals.

My investment philosophy (and the one I adhere to in my financial planning practice) is passive to the extent that I do not make judgements on the relative merits of one invest-ment over another, but I am not willing to accept the market rate (less fees) for my clients. My investment process targets market-beating performance through structured exposure to dimensions of higher expected return, and uses methods of portfolio construction and implementation that enhance performance relative to the average investor.

I believe:

- The average active investor will do worse than the market because they are paying the highest fees and that it is not possible to consistently beat the market through active management;

- The average index investor will perform slightly better than that because their fees are lower than the active investor; and
- My investment approach will outperform both due to reasonable fees, exposure to dimensions of higher expected return, and intelligent portfolio implementation.

There. That feels better. Now we know where I stand, let's attempt to answer the question:

What is Active Investing?

Active fund managers claim they can achieve superior returns to that of the market average and they charge investors a premium in the form of significantly higher management fees. However the vast majority of active fund managers fail to deliver on this promise and there is substantial academic research to support this.

The chances are you will obtain well below market returns over the lifetime of your plan if you choose active management as your preferred approach. There is however a lot of noise out there which the unwitting investor may find difficult to ignore.

This is because a whole industry has grown up around active investing and there are many active fund managers (with vested interests) in the city who are keen to perpetuate the myth that they can beat the market. The adverts these active funds place in the national press will almost always imply that they are the ones who can and do beat the market. There is, as I have said, however, overwhelming academic evidence to suggest that this is simply not the case some of which I intend to present to you here.

In his excellent book, *Index Funds*, Mark Hebner describes how active investors attempt to beat a market or benchmark by speculating on short term market fluctuations based on prediction and forecasting.

Active Investors' methods include:

- Identifying stocks expected to perform well in the future
- Moving in and out of industry sectors, or
- Attempting to time the market

Hebner further identifies the following characteristics of an active investor:

- Owning actively managed funds
- Picking Individual Stocks/Shares
- Choosing when to be in or out of the market
- Selecting a fund manager based on recent performance
- Ignoring high fees and commissions
- Investing without understanding the importance of long-term historical data

Hebner, in my opinion correctly, states that these methods rely on predicting the future direction of the economy, the stock market, or an individual stock while at the same time assuming it's possible to accurately predict the future. In his view, many people consider this to be the key to successful investing.

In fact, when people meet Financial Advisers or others in the investment business, their first question is typically, 'where do you think the market is going?' They are basically asking that person to make a prediction. Yet, no one can know the future — and if an investment person could predict the market's future direction, why would he share that knowledge for free?

But a prediction about an uncertain future is just an opinion. It should not determine anyone's investment decision.

Many people learn this the hard way. Active investors tend to ignore historical evidence in the belief that they can outsmart all the other investors in the market and beat a market or benchmark.

Many active investors also approach investing from an emotional perspective. They act impulsively—and their reaction is typically sparked by fear or greed. Some may get anxious about the stock market and decide to get out. This may ease their fear, but it may be replaced by the anxiety of missing out on a market recovery. Investors who flee the market ultimately have to decide when to get back in.

The 2008–09 global market downturn offers an example of how the cycle of fear and greed can drive an investor's decisions. Some investors fled the market in early 2009, just before the rebound began. They locked in their losses and then experienced the stress of watching the markets climb while they were out.

Every active fund manager's primary objective is to make a profit and so I would go so far as to say that they have their interests (and therefore, not necessarily yours) at heart, first and foremost. Of course, they want to make this profit so that you benefit from their gains and whilst they honestly believe that active investing is preferable to simply accepting average market returns, in the process they often develop complex or bespoke selection and trading systems. In my opinion, active investment management is more like a science than a trade. Its multi-levelled methodology requires the fund manager to analyse the results across a broad spectrum of data, in order to determine profitable future investment trends. All this hard work, all the software employed and investment in their business models costs money – ultimately, yours – and it's expensive to develop, maintain and execute. The commission fee they will deduct from you against trades funds their business – and not necessarily your retirement or any one of your goals.

But I do understand if you are, or have been, tempted to pursue an active investing plan of action. After all, the consumer financial media often screams at you from its headlines with sound bites that, on the surface, seem very persuasive.

'Timed to perfection – boost your returns
with methodical market timing'
Investor's Chronicle, 20/09/2013

'Bag yourself a share of this trillion-dollar payday'
Moneyweek, 04/04/2014

'Savers warned to watch how much money they pile into investments through new super ISAs'
This is Money, 04/04/2014

What is the alternative to active investing?

Passive investing

Unlike the active investment strategy, passive investment management doesn't discriminate between attractive or unattractive securities. Nor does it forecast securities prices, or time markets and market sectors. Instead passive investing is about using low cost index funds and or exchange traded funds (ETFs) to capture the market return from which a very small management fee is deducted

Don't get the wrong impression; just like active investors, passive investors still aim to make a profit. The big difference is they accept the average returns that the various asset classes produce. As I have mentioned, active investors face many more costs to justify the returns of the average passively managed portfolio. These costs include inflated management fees and trading and market impact costs, since active managers affect the prices they pay; dilution from maintaining higher cash positions than passive managers; more taxes in taxable accounts due to high turnover rates, and of course, their extra loaded commissions if an investment product, like a unit trust, is purchased through a third party such as a broker or financial salesperson. These cumulative costs create extra liabilities for the active investor, ranging from 1.5% - 10% per year, depending upon asset class mix, and whether a salesperson is involved. Even less expensive forms of active management, such as no-load mutual funds and wrap fee accounts, will still attract a minimum 1.3%-2.5% per year of an investor's returns.

On the other hand, the average passive or index portfolio is far more cost effective, usually under 0.4% per year. Therefore, active investing will cost the average investor more money with a far greater potential for failure than success. According to research quoted by Forbes in 2012 approximately 65% of active managers, as a group, underperform compared to passive portfolios during any given year and, over time, this percentage increases until only a tiny minority outperform market averages.

Why is the passive investment route more cost effective? Passive investors don't make use of all the scientific algorithms (and crystal balls for future forecasting) to inform their decisions and then they act accordingly when allocating their assets. The tools of their trade differ widely to active fund managers. Instead, they rely on long-term historical data that delineates probable asset class risks and returns, they make sure they diversify widely within and across the various asset classes and maintain allocations long-term through regular rebalancing.

Passive investing – no longer a big secret

It's only since 1973 when the acclaimed US economist, writer and Princeton Professor, Burton Malkiel, contended in his groundbreaking book, *A Random Walk Down Wall Street* that active investing was an underperforming methodology. As an early adopter of finding a way for ordinary people to own entire stock indexes he has been a strong promoter of passive investing, an approach which is gaining in popularity amongst investors and which is, according to forecasts by PWC, set to double by 2020 within the Exchange Traded Funds (ETF) sector. In the

US alone during 2014, investors switched over $80 billion from active funds and placed $60 billion into passive funds. That is because the market has soared in the last five years, but active fund managers haven't been able to keep pace. Passive investors, on the other hand, have reaped the rewards. According to CNN, anyone who bought an S&P 500 passively-managed index fund in early 2009 would have made three times their money. It's a compelling argument against active investing.

Another notable and respected exponent of passive investing is Richard Ferri whose book *The Power of Passive Investing* makes the case for why passive investing is a good choice for many investors, particularly those who do not have the time or financial expertise to compete with professional investors. It's detailed enough to really teach you things, yet easy to read enough that you don't need constant assistance in getting through the pages. Like my own book, it won't offer you specific advice; it is more about the how and why of passive investing, but it's a title that I would highly recommend.

John C. Bogel who founded the first index tracking fund company, Vanguard, in 1976 (and who is named one of the investment industry's four Giants of the 20th Century by

Fortune Magazine in 1999) endorses Ferri's stance when he writes in the book's foreword:

> An investor holding a portfolio of five equally weighted mutual funds has but a 3% probability of beating the stock market index over 25 years. (For a holder of ten funds, the probability is only 1%).

Ferri compares active investing using the analogy of playing the lottery, in that we are all tempted by the jackpot prizes. The big prize money is the headline grabbing incentive that persuades us to part with our money and to take part. But whilst the player is blinded by the thoughts of winning, in reality the *probability* of them winning that jackpot prize is almost nil since the odds are massively stacked against them. It's impossible to accurately predict the winning combination of numbers. The same is true with the markets and active investment fund managers can no sooner claim with any certainty that they can predict future market results in the same way nobody can predict the outcome of the lottery.

In my opinion, Burton Malkiel's findings in 1973 remain absolutely current and underpin my own philosophy towards the markets: that the investor who buys and holds a broadly based index fund and who effectively invests in the market as a whole, does better in the long run than all active investment fund managers do put together.

It's a message that Warren Buffet seems to agree with. There are still plenty of active investors who play the stock markets worldwide – indeed, they still carry out the majority of trades – but the passive investment trend is catching on. Don't let anyone try to convince you that passive investing is for couch potatoes only, or that you're not a real player of the stock market. With passive investing you still take risks – but only the ones that you are comfortable with because your investment portfolio and your risk profile are completely compatible. By choosing to passively invest – as history has shown - you are far more likely to achieve your goals not to mention get a better night's sleep!

Chapter 9

Behave Yourself

By this point in the book you should already have decided upon a suitable asset allocation and diversified your investments between a wide selection of stocks and bonds. In this chapter I am talking about the stocks/equity component of your portfolio as although bonds will also fluctuate in value they are likely to be less volatile than equities.

The key concept to take away from this chapter is that your behaviour is by far and away the most significant factor in determining the long-term performance of your investment portfolio.

Investors are usually their own worst enemy

Taking control of your emotions and controlling your own behaviour is easier said than done. However, if you can master them the rewards are likely to be substantial and will lead you to achieve superior investment returns, the like of which the average investor will never experience.

In this chapter I am going to be talking about long-term investing and the mind-set you need to have to be successful as a long-term investor. There will always be people who believe (even those who have read the previous chapter and the active vs passive debate) that they can get to their goals faster by choosing the best funds or individual equities for their portfolio or by timing when to be in or out of the market. This book is not for those people. I can assure you there is overwhelming evidence that this approach doesn't work for the vast majority of mere mortals – myself included. The higher costs you will incur by attempting to beat the market make this approach like trying to win a motor race with your handbrake on the whole way and as we have already discussed no one can consistently time the market.

It cannot be overstated how important it is to stay disciplined in the face of adversity. There will be volatility at times in the economic cycle. Accept this. It is the price you have to pay for superior returns.

Another major benefit of investing in the manner I am outlining in this chapter is that you will not suffer the sleepless nights of the average investor. Investing will become an almost stress-free experience. Since I am an advocate of maintaining your health (both physical and emotional) the last thing you need to be doing is to fall into a blind panic on waking in the morning and turning on the news to hear that there has been a slide in the market. In my opinion, that's absolutely not the right way to invest. What I say is, just let the market work its magic, hang in there, stay true to your plan and have the discipline to rebalance your portfolio at the regular intervals you have committed to. That's how you will achieve way above average returns on your investments by staying in the market long term.

You would not plant a tree and then pull it up every few months to see how fast it was growing and then replant it somewhere else in your garden. It's the same with your portfolio.

We've already explored in the previous chapter the key components of constructing a long-term investment plan. You now owe it to yourself to allow your investments the chance to work their magic over time.

This won't always be easy. Humans are emotional beings and the temptation to do something in a stock market downturn will sometimes feel almost irresistible. But logic tells us you must get control of your emotions if you are not to join the masses of average investors who receive mediocre returns at best and suffer tremendous amounts of unnecessary stress. It's during these stressful times that you will perhaps be more susceptible to the headlines in the financial press on Sunday mornings with its 'buy this new hot fund' or 'now is not a good time to buy gold' etc. This is just noise and nothing else. You must be vigilant in the face of such temptation to tinker with your portfolio. You must be able to shut out this media noise, and act in a counter-intuitive manner - I make no apologies for reinforcing this point over and over again.

You may be new to investing and the market's volatile nature – it's one thing to hear about the FTSE 100's daily ups and downs on the TV news every day, but it's another thing when you literally are invested in it. Which is why I have longed to pass on the benefit of my experience as a Financial Advisor in a book such as this. There is overwhelming evidence that you cannot time the market; those investors who do best are those who stay in for the long term and regularly rebalance their portfolio.

This does not, however, stop the media/active fund management industry from trying to convince you otherwise.

Just in the last 12 months I have heard comments from active fund managers such as 'we are holding an over-weight cash position as we are expecting volatility ahead of the Scottish Independence vote' (the vote took place in September 2014) and 'We recommend waiting until after the situation in Greece has been resolved before you make a withdrawal from your portfolio'. They would have us believe that they know something we mere mortals don't. Many investors find this perfectly plausible, so they happily carry on paying their high fees.

Well, I'm here to tell you that these sorts of comments are pure speculation and reacting to the latest news story in this way is likely to be seriously detrimental to your wealth!

As I have mentioned, it's not just the active fund managers who spin these stories. Pick up a Sunday newspaper and you will find advertisements for investments that talk about recent short-term performance or star fund managers focussing on the performance of their flagship fund whilst conveniently ignoring their other not-so-great funds. Even if you did buy into the star manager argument, ask yourself how many of the superstars of 10 years ago are still per-forming today. The big fund management groups regularly launch new funds and will spend large sums on placing tempting advertisements to catch your eye with their promises of potentially higher returns. But what they don't like to advertise is that a few years later, half those funds are nowhere to be seen because they haven't performed nearly as well as they claimed they might. Occasionally one of the funds performs exceedingly well but in all honesty, this is more by luck than by judgement. But that's the one that they will herald with great fanfare when they advertise the next new fund to tempt you. Do not be tempted!

It's obvious by my tone that I am highly critical of the financial press and how it targets potential investors who have worked hard for their money and who are considering the available options to enjoy it in your retirement. How many times have you picked up a financial magazine aimed at investors offering weekly tips on what to buy, hold or sell? I have already outlined that this is a sure-fire way to do badly because you're going to keep incurring more costs every time you trade – costs that will deplete your available funds and with no guarantee of success. Often these sell tips are advising you to sell funds/shares they recommended you buy only a year or two ago! There will always be a perfectly plausible accompanying explanation as to why it didn't work out – this time.

Effectively all this noise is encouraging turnover in your investment portfolio by speculating on timing i.e. 'now's a great time to buy XYZ fund' and stock picking i.e. 'ABC looks undervalued at the moment'.

To reiterate, the best way to become a successful investor is to hold for the long term, buy low and sell high, and follow a disciplined re-balancing process such as I recommended in Chapter 7.

It is however human nature to want to hang on to invest-ments that have gone up in value and dump those that have remained static or, worse still, fallen in value. Once again I have to urge you to resist this temptation as this type of tinkering will almost certainly lead to vastly inferior returns.

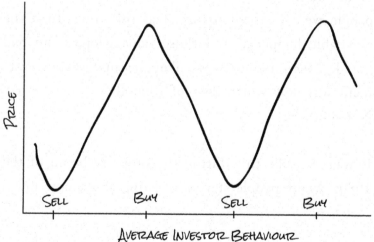

AVERAGE INVESTOR BEHAVIOUR

This graph shows how the average investor will tend to sit on the side-lines in a rising market until euphoria reaches an all-time high. Eventually, as the market is close to its peak, even their pals at the golf club are talking about how well their share portfolio is doing. It is at this time that they now decide they need to join the gravy train because they can't afford to miss out any longer. Of course we all know what happens next – there is a market correction, share prices fall and our newbie investor panics saying to themselves 'I can't afford to lose any more money'. They then sell out at a substantial loss.

Remember the tech stocks boom in the late 90s? It was hard to avoid people bragging about how their technology fund was up by 100% in just two years. Many people were tempted to invest at this time. Then the inevitable happened and those same people who had doubled their money were silent because their investment was now worth 25% of what they had invested. Not good!

It was also like this during the property boom of the 1980s. Many people started boasting about how much money they made on their property by simply sitting back and waiting for the values to increase. It was a favourite topic of dinner conversation – yawn... First-time buyers were flooding into the property market believing that if they didn't buy now they might never be able to. This is because they believed property was a sure thing (by the way it usually is if you hold it long enough, which makes you wonder why people don't apply this same logic to their equity portfolios) and that the price could only ever go up. Eventually there was a massive correction and property prices fell (my own home fell by 40% in value between 1989 and 1992) and took almost 10 years to recover. Some people handed their keys back to their lenders during this period and ended up with a debt they couldn't afford to pay back. The key to success was once again to stay with it. Those who held on, or better still started buying some investment properties while the prices were at ridiculously low levels, did very well once prices did recover. I was one of those people. I couldn't sell my home at a loss and although I wanted to move (I had a growing family by then) I stayed put and instead started to acquire a little portfolio of bargain properties to let (there was no shortage of people preferring to rent at this time). I made some handsome profits, more than compensating for the drop in value on my main residence, but I can still remember friends and family telling me I was 'mad' to buy property at this time as it would never recover.

I relay this personal story not to brag but just to emphasise the importance of doing the opposite of what the majority are doing. Follow your own plan and shut out the noise and don't take advice from anyone who is not a successful investor themselves.

In his book 'Behavioural Investment Counselling' Nick Murray offers a sobering example of the cost of behaving like an average investor when he makes reference to a Lipper & Dalton study which shows the disparity between the compounded average return on the average US large cap equity mutual fund vs. the return achieved by the average equity mutual fund investor for the 20 years to 2007:

Average US Equity Fund	Average US Equity Fund Investor
10.81% per annum	4.48% per annum

These figures, derived from a study carried out in the USA don't, in fact, differ much from the UK It doesn't really matter which 20 year period you look at (on both sides of the Atlantic) the outcome is pretty much the same – average investors achieve less than half the annual return of investors who simply buy and hold.

To obtain this dramatic outperformance all the investor would have had to do was to buy the average fund, not the star performer (no-one knows which one that will be anyway) and do nothing but hold it.

Over the 20 years there would have been significant ups and downs and he would have had to resist the temptation to tinker, but do this and 'Bob's your uncle'. In 20 years he would have achieved double the compound return of the average, 'tinkerer' investor! But there will always be people in that marketplace who want to ignore the facts and who will try to convince you otherwise. Yet the indisputable facts clearly show that you don't have to listen to, or aspire to be, a city whizz kid and that by slowly marinating your portfolio of average performing funds you are very likely to outperform your active investor counterparts by up to 60% and sometimes more.

Investment discipline

The investor's chief problem – and even
his worst enemy – is likely to be himself.

Benjamin Graham —*Security Analysis,* **1934**

In *An Owner's Manual,* distributed to Berkshire Hathaway shareholders in 1996, Warren Buffett wrote:

> Do not think of yourself as merely owning a piece of paper whose price wiggles around daily and that is a candidate for sale when some economic or political event makes you nervous. Instead visualize yourself as a part owner of a business that you expect to stay with indefinitely, much as you might if you owned a farm or apartment house in partnership with members of your family.

This, in my opinion, is seriously good advice. If his net worth, according to *Forbes* (July 2015) was not in excess of $65bn perhaps his viewpoint would more open to question. Unlike the other wealthy people on *Forbes'* Top 10 Rich List, Buffett doesn't own an oil well or a retail empire, or a multinational corporation – he simply owns a huge amount of share certificates. The world's third richest man has made his fortune through buying shares in companies that he believed were worth more than their market value and by investing in them for the long-term. Even though his wealth is eye watering compared to most people's, nevertheless, we can all learn from his strategy.

If you're thinking 'but 20 years is too long and I don't want to invest for that long' remember the average retirement now lasts 30 years and sometimes 40. Your investments need to last a lifetime and with recent changes in legislation (to pensions in particular) more and more people will be passing on this wealth to the next generation. This means the term of your investment might run to 60 years or more!

Consistency beats volatility

For most investors, when a professional Financial Adviser cautions discipline, they interpret this as meaning: stick with the programme through good times and the bad. But in actual fact, it's when the markets have experienced exceptionally good investment returns, such as the dot com phenomenon of the late 1990s as opposed to significant downturns that proved the greater challenge in maintaining any kind of strategy.

I would like to leave you with this one, final thought. If you ever find yourself doubting your decision to invest passively, as opposed to actively investing, and you feel pressurised by your peers or the financial media into divesting yourself of your couch potato, or dull portfolio, take a step backwards and remember this: when it comes to investing, boring is good and it will win out almost every time in the long term.

I hope this book has been of great benefit to you in clarifying your future plans and it is my personal wish that it has inspired you to take action to start living the life of your dreams. Always remember One Day truly is Now!

I hope that you now – as Mr. Spock would say, 'live long and prosper'.

The Author

For Martin Turbin, helping people
make the most of the assets they've
accumulated is rewarding work.
Martin enjoys guiding his clients as
they implement the financial strategies that help them achieve their
goals.

As Founder and CEO of Turbin Wealth Management,
Martin adopts a comprehensive approach to wealth
management. He sees his role as helping people make
smart decisions about their investments and retirement
plans – providing them with a greater financial independence, peace of mind and security.

With more than 25 years' experience in the financial planning profession, Martin has a wealth of real world experience in advising clients at critical stages in their lives
(particularly retirement). He was one of the first financial planners in the United Kingdom to begin providing
cashflow modelling for clients before 'financial planning'
became widely known as a profession. As a Lifestyle

Financial Planner (a kind of "life coach" who specialises in money), he has demonstrated a consistent ability to protect and grow the hard-earned assets of his clients, many of whom have experienced major life changes including retirement, divorce or the loss of a spouse.

Martin is one of only a small number of UK advisers to hold the elite Certified Financial Planner^{cm} Practitioner designation (CFP^{cm}) and is a member of the Institute of Financial Planning (IFP) and Personal Finance society (PFS).

Martin values education as a way to promote professional excellence and over the years has facilitated a number of educational seminars for solicitors and accountants with whom he often collaborates to provide a holistic financial plan for his clients.

When he's not in the office, Martin enjoys playing tennis, travelling and spending time with his wife, Carol and their three adult children.

If you'd like to learn more about how Martin and his team can help you, visit www.turbin.co.uk and get in touch.

Lightning Source UK Ltd.
Milton Keynes UK
UKOW01f2203030917
308474UK00003B/63/P